THE
PHILOSOPHICAL
HITCHCOCK

THE
PHILOSOPHICAL
HITCHCOCK

Vertigo and the Anxieties of Unknowingness

ROBERT B. PIPPIN

THE UNIVERSITY OF CHICAGO PRESS   CHICAGO AND LONDON

The University of Chicago Press, Chicago 60637
The University of Chicago Press, Ltd., London
© 2017 by The University of Chicago
All rights reserved. No part of this book may be used or reproduced in any manner whatsoever without written permission, except in the case of brief quotations in critical articles and reviews. For more information, contact the University of Chicago Press, 1427 E. 60th St., Chicago, IL 60637.
Published 2017
Printed in the United States of America

26 25 24 23 22 21 20 19 18 17   1 2 3 4 5

ISBN-13: 978-0-226-50364-6 (cloth)
ISBN-13: 978-0-226-50378-3 (e-book)
DOI: 10.7208/chicago/9780226503783.001.0001

Library of Congress Cataloging-in-Publication Data

Names: Pippin, Robert B., 1948– author.
Title: The philosophical Hitchcock : Vertigo and the anxieties of unknowingness / Robert B. Pippin.
Description: Chicago ; London : The University of Chicago Press, 2017. | Includes bibliographical references and index.
Identifiers: LCCN 2017001242 | ISBN 9780226503646 (cloth : alk. paper) | ISBN 9780226503783 (e-book)
Subjects: LCSH: Vertigo (Motion picture : 1958) | Philosophy in motion pictures.
Classification: LCC PN1995.9.P42 P56 2017 | DDC 791.43/72—dc23 LC record available at https://lccn.loc.gov/2017001242

♾ This paper meets the requirements of ANSI/NISO Z39.48-1992 (Permanence of Paper).

In memory of Victor Perkins

You sort of forget you're you. —Emmy, *Shadow of a Doubt*

It's quite remarkable to discover that one isn't what one thought one was. —Dr. Peterson, *Spellbound*

Who comes to seek the living among the dead? —Luke 24:5

CONTENTS

ACKNOWLEDGMENTS

I began writing this book while teaching a summer seminar in Switzerland with my friend and colleague Jim Conant, and I finished it sometime after we had taught a course together at the University of Chicago on Hitchcock's American films. I want to express my thanks to Professor Katia Saporiti of the University of Zurich for the invitation to deliver the seminar, and to the participants in the seminar for our lively discussions. I am yet again, as with my other two books about film, very grateful to Jim for our conversations about Hitchcock, film aesthetics, and much else over the last twenty years.

I have also had the privilege of presenting material from this book in lectures at Beloit College, Johns Hopkins, the University of Chicago, Northwestern, Berkeley, and Stanford. The discussions after the lectures were invariably lively, thoughtful, and very helpful, and I thank those audiences. I have also been helped by generous comments from Dan Morgan, Wendy Doniger, Mark Jenkins, Paul Kottman, and the late Victor Perkins, and by a number of acute comments from Fred Rush.

I wrote the final draft over part of the summer at a farmhouse in the Hudson River Valley. I am happy to express how very much I have gained from frequent conversations there about the film and related matters with Michael Fried and Ruth Leys, and how grateful I am for their valuable comments and for their friendship.

This book is dedicated to the memory of Victor Perkins, who died in July of 2016. I had been a dedicated admirer of Victor's work on film since

I first read *Film as Film* many years ago, and I then read everything else he wrote. I got to know him personally about a decade ago in Chicago, and we stayed in touch after that through correspondence and occasional meetings, in Warwick and then for the last time in Munich. We shared a love for Nicholas Ray, Max Ophüls, and Hitchcock, among others, and he was always as generous and insightful a correspondent about drafts of articles and general issues as anyone I have ever known. He was also among the most humane, kind, and forthright people I have ever met. To say of someone that he was a "lovely person" can sound quite indeterminate, but anyone who had the great good fortune to have known Victor will know exactly what I mean.

White Oak House
Buskirk, New York
July 2016

PROLOGUE: FILM AND PHILOSOPHY

As the book title indicates, I am proposing a philosophical reading of Hitch-cock's *Vertigo*. My goal is to offer an interpretation that shows how the film can be said to bear on a philosophical problem, the problem I set out in this and the following section. This proposal immediately involves two enor-mous questions: what philosophy is, such that a film could be said to bear on it; and how an art object, a film in particular, must be conceived such that it could intersect with, bear on, philosophy. Several other unmanage-able questions immediately arise. Stanley Cavell has said that what serious thought about great film requires is "humane criticism dealing with whole films,"[1] and he later calls such criticism "readings." But what are readings of films, especially "philosophical" readings?[2]

To try to address such questions in an opening section and then move on would obviously be foolish. But, given the proposal, some statement of principles (and nothing like a defense of the principles) is in order. So I briefly offer a summary of such commitments, but only that.

Consider first the conditions that must obtain for a cinematic experi-ence to be an *aesthetic* experience, an experience uniquely directed at, in-

---

1. Stanley Cavell, *The World Viewed: Reflections on the Ontology of Film* (Cambridge, MA: Harvard University Press, 1979), 12.
2. Cavell, *The World Viewed*, 9: "I do not deny that there is a problem about the idea of 'reading a movie.' Is it greater, or other, than the problem about the idea of 'reading a poem,' when, of course, that is not the same as reciting the poem?"

formed by, a work of art. When we are attending to a work as a work of art, we could not be doing so unless we knew that this is what we are doing. Not all filmed narratives are works of art. There are home movies, orientation videos, documentary recordings, surveillance tapes, and so forth, and except in extremely unusual circumstances, we know when we are experiencing a filmed fictional narrative. An aesthetic experience does not simply happen to someone. It requires a particular mode of attending. This knowing-we-are-so-attending is nothing like a self-observation, an attending to oneself as an object. It is a constituting aspect of *aesthetic attending itself*, not a separate noting of that fact. It is in attending *this way* that we are, in George Wilson's terms, "imaginatively seeing" what we are seeing.[3] Or, at least, this is how I understand his claim, not how he puts it. That is, we are not seeing actors on a big screen and, in a second step, imagining them being fictional characters (that is how he puts it).

It is also not the case that attending aesthetically — of knowing what we are doing when we are experiencing, attending to, the work — is something that interferes with or competes with our direct emotional absorption in the plot. We can start watching a movie with the assumption that its ambition is merely to entertain us; we thus attend to it in such a way, take ourselves to be having such an experience. But then someone points out for us that there are elements in the movie that might be entertaining but also raise questions beyond plot details, questions that cannot be explained by that function alone. We then attend to the movie in a different way, a way I want to follow Wilson in continuing to call imaginative seeing, or, in the terms used above, aesthetically attending, but which now also requires interpretive work. We don't, in such a case, lose interest in the plot and become interested in another issue. (The same sort of "parallel track attending" is possible in admiring the performance of an actor even as we follow and try to understand what the character is doing. The main point is the same. There are not two steps: seeing the actor and imagining the character.)[4] We realize there are aspects of the film "we have not understood." We

---

3. George Wilson, *Seeing Fictions in Film: The Epistemology of Movies* (Oxford: Oxford University Press, 2011).

4. This is no more mysterious than our concentrating on the promises being made in the marriage exchange, while aware that it is by saying them, in this context, with the right authority present, that we *are* thereby marrying. That is, it is not mysterious at all.

can say, then, that the imagination or attending in question is not limited to an emotional involvement in the events we see (and in what might happen) and in the events and motivations in the world of the film, but it ranges over many elements, as we try also to imagine *why* we are shown things just this way. When that happens, we attend aesthetically in a different register, see imaginatively, an attending that now includes an interpretive task.

Giving a formulaic account of just what in the work "demands" such closer interpretive attending is not easy. At least it is hard to point to anything beyond this abstract appeal to "questions raised by the work," which are not questions about plot details but are questions like, Why are we so often looking from below at figures in shadows in some film noir? Or, What does it mean that Gary Cooper's character throws his marshal's badge to the ground in obvious disgust at the end of *High Noon* (1952)? Or, Why does the director "twin" Grace Kelly's wedding ring with that badge? Or, Why is Hitchcock so apparently indifferent to the obvious artificiality, the blatant, even comic phoniness of the back projection techniques he uses frequently in *Marnie* (1964)? It is even more difficult to present a general account of when those questions are distinctly philosophical in character.

The very idea of some fruitful intersection between film and philosophy remains a controversial one. Many academics who think and write about film, and a great many philosophers of all kinds, would dispute this view. No one can deny that interesting philosophical questions can be raised about film, such as questions about the nature of the medium, its distinctness as an art form, the nature of cinematic experience, its relation to theater and painting, and so forth. It is the idea that a film (or a novel or a poem) itself can be understood as a form of thought, especially a form of philosophical thought, that is not widely accepted. And this is an especially vexed issue for a special reason. One of philosophy's chief topics is itself and the endlessly contested question of what philosophy is, whether there even is such a practice. Asking this sort of question about film puts us at the center of such centuries-old disputes. The idea of a film, novel, or poem as a form of philosophical thought is more recognizable among philosophers in the historical tradition who themselves had something close to this "complementary" view about philosophy and the arts, primarily but not exclusively philosophy and literature. Examples include Hegel's treatment of Sophocles or Diderot in his *Phenomenology of Spirit*, Kierkegaard's use of *Don Giovanni*, Schopenhauer's theory of the philosophical significance of music, Nietzsche's reflections on Greek tragedy and an "aesthetic justification of existence," and Heidegger's appeal to Hölderlin. In the case of Hegel, for example, art in general, together with religion and philosophy, is treated as part of a collective attempt at self-knowledge over time, and is viewed not as a competitor with religion or philosophy but as a different and indispensable way (a sensible and affective way according to Hegel) of pursuing such a goal. The notion is also not foreign to philosophers influenced by Wittgenstein, concerned with, as it is put, how we came to be in the grip of a picture of, say, the mind's relation to the world, or our relation to each other, and how we might be "shown" how to escape that picture. (This is especially so with Cavell's work, concerned as he is with various dimensions of skepticism and given his view that film is "the moving image of skepticism.")[5] The central question in Heidegger's work, the meaning of being, a question about meaning in the existential not linguistic sense, is understandably a question that might be informed by how such a meaning might be "disclosed," as Heidegger sometimes puts it, in a work of art.

However large and contested the topic, if this notion of "philosophic work" in film is to have some currency, we need a clearer idea of what might distinguish a "philosophical reading" of a film, and how such a reading might contribute something to philosophy itself.

As suggested above, we are sometimes prompted to ask what the director—or the collective intelligence we can postulate behind the making of the film—meant by so narrating the tale we are following.[6] We want

---

5. Stanley Cavell, *Pursuits of Happiness: The Hollywood Comedy of Remarriage* (Cambridge, MA.: Harvard University Press, 1981), 188–89.

6. I am adopting the so-called fictional or as-if narrator position, an implication of which is that the attribution of intentions to such a narrator has nothing to do with what some historical individual, e.g., the director, actually had in mind. I am in agreement here with what Stanley Cavell says about an "artist's intention" in his discussion of whether Fellini can be said "to have intended" a reference to the Philomel myth in *La Strada*. See Cavell, "A Matter of Meaning It," in *Must We Mean What We Say* (Cambridge: Cambridge University Press, 1976), 230–31. It also is important to understand something that the philosopher of film George Wilson stresses: this narrator should be conceived in cinematically minimalist terms. The agency of such a narrator "is merely minimal, i.e., generally invisible and inaudible to the spectator, uniformly effaced, and characteristically inexpressive." Wilson, *Seeing Fictions in Films* (Oxford: Oxford University Press, 2011), 129. "Characteristically" is the key word here. Our attention can be explicitly directed to the fact of narration by the director, something quite

to know the point of showing us such a story at all, and showing it to us in just this way, with just this selection of shots, from which point of view at what point in the film, with just this selection of detail. In the same way that we could say that we understood perfectly some sentence said to us by someone, but that we cannot understand the point of his saying it now, here, in this context, given what we had been discussing, we could also say that we can understand some complex feature of a movie plot, but wonder what the point might have been in showing us this feature in such a way in that context.

This allows me to put the point in an even broader way. Visualized fictional narratives, movies, can be said to have many functions, can be said to "do" or accomplish various things.[7] They please, for example, or they are painful to watch, but painful in some odd way that is pleasant as well. We can also say, in a straightforward, commonsense way, that some films can be means of rendering ourselves intelligible to each other, rendering some feature of human life more intelligible than it otherwise would have been. This can be as simple as a clearer recognition that, say, some aspect of the implications of a violation of trust *is* as it is shown. This might require in some cinematic presentation of this drama, a narrative about a decision to trust in a situation of great uncertainty,[8] and this narrative might show us what is generally involved in such a decision, and what "follows" from the violation, what "backshadowing" effects it has, what it portends for the fu-

---

prominent, say, at the beginning of *Psycho* (1960), with its expansive, searching pan (from no point of view that could be occupied by anyone in the film) and an intrusive, "spying" descent through an open window. For a longer discussion of Wilson's thesis, see Robert Pippin, "Le grand imagier of George Wilson," *European Journal of Philosophy* 21, no. 2 (Summer 2013): 334–41. Finally, for the notion that there is great narrative complexity in classic Hollywood cinema, I (and I would think, everyone else) is indebted to the pathbreaking work of V. S. Perkins, *Film as Film: Understanding and Judging Movies* (New York: Penguin Books, 1972), esp. 9–27; and George Wilson, *Narration in Light: Studies in Cinematic Point of View* (Baltimore: Johns Hopkins University Press, 1986), esp. 1–15.

7. For another discussion of this point, framed in these terms but focused on another and very specific example, see Robert Pippin, "Minds in the Dark: Cinematic Experience in the Dardenne Brothers' *Dans l'obscurité*," *nonsite.org*, no. 19 (Spring 2016), http://nonsite.org/article/minds-in-the-dark-2.

8. Think of Robert Bresson's *A Man Escaped* (1956), where the main character, Fontaine, must decide whether to trust a young man whom Fontaine does not know well at all if his escape plan is to work. He must trust not only the man, but his own judgment, one based on a sense of a brief, epiphanic insight. We come to realize that in all of this the question of faith, the meaning and implications of faith, is being raised.

ture, all in a way that a brief philosophical example in a discursive account could not. Now, if the question is what the director (or, again, the collective intelligence we can postulate behind the making of the film) meant *by* so narrating a tale, sometimes the answer will certainly be that he, or she, or they, meant only *to be narrating* the tale, because the tale is in itself entertaining, thrilling, hilarious. But some films can be said to attempt to illuminate something about human conduct that would otherwise remain poorly understood. The point or purpose of such narrating seems to be such an illumination. There is some point of view taken and not another; and so there is an implicit saying that some matter of significance, perhaps some philosophical or moral or political issue, is "like *this*," thereby saying that it is "not like *that*." And one other way of rendering intelligible or illuminating is to show that what we might have thought unproblematic or straightforward is not that at all, and is much harder to understand than we often take for granted. Coming to see that something is not as intelligible as we had thought can also be revealing. (Bernard Williams once wrote that there can be a great difference between what we actually think about something and "what we merely think that we think,"[9] and great literature or great film can make clear to us in a flash, sometimes to our discomfort, what we really think. In the same way that a film noir's credibility and illuminating power might throw into doubt that we ever really know our own minds, and so can challenge what many philosophical theories assume.[10] Hitchcock's *Vertigo* might disturb settled, commonsense views about what it is to understand another person or be understood by him or her, or about how we present ourselves to others in our public personae.)

If at least part of what happens to us when we watch a film is that events and dialogues are not just present to us but are shown to us, and if the question this fact raises—what is the point of showing us this narrative in this way?—does not in some cases seem fully answered by purposes like pleasure or entertainment, because something of a far more general, philosophical significance is intimated, some means of understanding something better, that all of this occurs in an aesthetic register, in our attending

9.   Bernard Williams, *Shame and Necessity* (Berkeley: University of California Press, 1993), 7.
10.   See Robert Pippin, *Fatalism in American Film Noir: Some Cinematic Philosophy* (Charlottesville: University of Virginia Press, 2012).

aesthetically to what is shown, then that much larger question, of a film's philosophical significance, with philosophy understood in some sort of traditional way, is obvious. This issue is, admittedly, quite a specific one. Movies also enter a complex social world, charged with issues of hierarchy, power, gender roles, social class, and many other fields of significance, and they can also come to mean a variety of things (across historical times) to different audiences in ways never anticipated by the makers of the film.[11] But one perspective need not exclude others, and the test for any perspective is the quality of the readings that result from looking at a film one way rather than another, readings that stay in close touch with the films. Not that it plays any prominent role in what follows, but I am taking my bearings from the way art came to matter to philosophy in Hegel's philosophy and in the tradition that philosophy inspired,[12] and I am happy to let everything ride on whether some illuminating sense can be made of this one film within such a perspective. So I concentrate on the reading and not the theoretical background.

Such an approach faces an obvious problem already noted that must be addressed at least briefly. How could such a visualized fictional narrative, concerning such *particular* fictional persons and particular fictional events, even or especially when marked out by an aspiration that is aesthetic, bear any *general* significance? Generality, we know, is a matter of form, and it is possible at least to imagine that the events we see are instances, perhaps highly typical and especially illuminating instances, of some general form of human relatedness.[13] Shakespeare, for example, would not be able to

---

11.   Of particular interest in recent years are feminist approaches to the films. Hitchcock's representation of female characters obviously expressed quite a complicated, somewhat tortured, sometimes anxious, and sometimes even hostile relation to women, allowing him to be portrayed as a misogynist, as a feminist avant la lettre, and more simply as someone simply terrified of women (an attitude he makes Cary Grant's characters themselves express twice, in *Notorious* [1946] and in *North by Northwest* [1959]). See Tania Modleski, *The Women Who Knew Too Much: Hitchcock and Feminist Theory* (New York: Methuen, 1988); and, for a sense of the terms of the debate, or what those terms have now become, Tania Modleski, "Remastering the Master: Hitchcock after Feminism," in *New Literary History* 47, no. 1 (Winter 2016): 135–58.

12.   A programmatic statement of such an approach can be found in Robert Pippin, *After the Beautiful: Hegel and the Philosophy of Pictorial Modernism* (Chicago: University of Chicago Press, 2013).

13.   In this case, I mean the generality of philosophy as a discourse, roughly in the sense evoked by Aristotle's famous comparison between poetry and history. But another inflection of the issue

portray so well Othello's jealousy unless the origins and conditions and implications of jealousy itself were also somehow at issue, shown to us in however particular a case. But how might such a level of generality be intimated by a narrative with a very concrete, particular plot, and what would explain the illumination's relation to some truth, not to mere psychological effectiveness? (A film after all can be powerfully compelling, can suggest an ambition to reach this level of generality, and, if the director is technically talented, can carry us along with this point of view, only for us on reflection to realize that the point of view we had initially accepted is in fact infantile, cartoonish, pandering to the adolescent fantasies of its mostly male fans.)

This example suggests a set of further examples that are recognizable philosophical questions but do not seem to admit of anything like Socratic definitions, or necessary and sufficient conditions for their having the determinate meaning they do. Many involve so-called thick concepts that require a great deal of interpretive finesse to understand whether the concept is even applicable, and how we might know in some complicated context or other whether it is relevant at all. I mean moral issues like, Does this count as a violation of trust? Should that consequence have been foreseen? In this particular situation of wrongdoing, who (if anyone) is morally blameworthy and why? When rightly blaming someone, when is it wrong to *keep* blaming him or her? Who might *seem* to be, but finally not be, blamable? How does such seeming and distinguishing work? What does forgiveness require before it is reasonably granted? (Is it ever reasonably granted, or is it beyond reasons?) Who, under what conditions, is worthy of trust, and who is not? How would one decide that? What is an acceptable risk in exposing oneself to betrayal or manipulation? Can the same action be said to be at the same time both good and evil, noble and ignoble, loving and self-interested? Is the relation between such value contraries not one of opposition, but gradations, as Nietzsche claimed?[14] What would that *look*

---

occurs in literary or film criticism itself, and has to do with the process of possible "identification" of a particular reader with, somehow, a particular character. Or not. See Frances Ferguson's discussion, "Now It's Personal: D. A. Miller and Too-Close Reading," in *Critical Inquiry* 41, no. 3 (Spring 2015): 521–40, esp. the pithy summary on 539–40. The issue, as posed this way, is a kind of psychological puzzle. The philosophical issue is a problem posed at a different register, one I discuss as the general *point* of the narration.

14.   Friedrich Nietzsche, *Beyond Good and Evil: Prelude to a Philosophy of the Future*, trans. J. Norman (Cambridge: Cambridge University Press, 2002), §24 and §25.

like? In what ways might all such issues look different in different communities at different times?[15]

And there are issues raised by some films, questions we seem to confront in trying to understand the films, in what has come to be called moral psychology. How do people come to understand what they are doing; what act description, in some contestable context, is rightly self-ascribed? Why do they often wrongly, and sometimes culpably wrongly, understand what they are doing? Or, in other words, how is self-deceit possible? And again, a question that could be asked as a corollary to each of these: What does that phenomenon *look* like? What do we detect when we think we detect the presence of self-deceit, as opposed to deliberate fraudulence, or a lack of self-knowledge? How do we make ourselves intelligible to each other, especially when desire and self-interest make that very hard to do? How do we figure each other out, and why, in the most important situations of love, danger, and trust, do we often seem to be so bad at it? What is romantic love; that is, does it exist, or it a dangerous fantasy? And do we know it when we see it? How important is it in a human life? What is the best, the most admirable, way to live with, to bear the burden of, the knowledge that we face eternal nonexistence, death? What distinguishes how we live now from how we used to live? Is how we live now a good way to live? What is objectionable about it? If a movie can, speaking very informally, "shed light" on such issues, then is there a limited but potentially important *kind* of illumination: primarily by means of filmed photographs moving in time?

As noted, what a film must do to achieve a perspective that is more than one focused on a filmed narrative of a particular fictional character, a fictional case study, is reach some level of general significance, one where these general notions themselves are in play and in some way posed to the viewer. The basic idea of the pertinence of drama to philosophy is as old as Aristotle's claim in his *Poetics* that drama is more philosophical than history because of the generalities and probabilities suggested, and

---

15.   The need for such interpretive finesse puts us close to the territory opened up by the pioneer in modern aesthetics, Kant, and his account of the distinctive "free play" of the imagination in the aesthetic experience of "concepts" like those listed in this paragraph. The point is strengthened if we say, as I think we should, that there is no better, perhaps no other, way to understand such phenomena than through such a guided but not regulated imaginative reflection.

as relatively recent as Hegel's notion of the "concrete universal," an instance that best expresses its kind, revealing the kind's essence much better than an abstract definition. The question is how such generality can be intimated.

One way such a level of generality can be suggested is by the relation of the film to other films, to films by other directors, referenced in a manner that suggests the general thematic purposiveness of that director's overall project, and especially by reference to the filmmaker's other films, directly suggesting again such a commonality and so generality of purpose. At some point such repetitions and similarities can suggest a sort of mythic universality.[16] That is certainly true of Hitchcock's films. There is something like a "Hitchcock world," a set of problems repeatedly faced by his characters, many having to do with the painfulness and the dangers of our general failure to understand ourselves or each other very well, or to make effective use of what little we do understand to direct our actions accordingly, all as recognizable as the formal cinematic markers of what is called, what he himself called, his "style." With the issues set out like this, we can ask about that world the claim to truth that its representation makes on us, and the particular emphasis given to several of its typical features in what many, certainly what I, would consider his masterpiece, the 1958 film *Vertigo*. This is a particularly difficult issue in that film since it seems to be about *quite* a distinct individual, a neurotic with vertigo caused by acrophobia obsessed with a woman who is impersonating another woman. What could be more idiosyncratically unique than such a tale? Could anything of any general significance follow from answering the question, What is the point of *Vertigo*? What is the point of showing us just this narration in just this way? I suggest it has a great deal to do with, let us call it, a general, common struggle for *mutual interpretability* in a social world where that becomes increasingly difficult and increasingly vital, both for the pursuit of our own interests and for the stability and security of our friendships and romantic relationships. The film can be said to explore *why* it is a struggle; what kind of society makes such failure more likely,

16. For a fuller discussion, see Robert Pippin, *Hollywood Westerns and American Myth: The Importance of Howard Hawks and John Ford for Political Philosophy* (New Haven, CT: Yale University Press, 2012).

and why; how and especially why we so often manage to get in our own way in such attempts; what, mostly by implication, would count as success in such a struggle and how it might be achieved. Such a nondiscursive treatment of aspects of human irrationality can be said to be attempting to show us the "nature" of these phenomena, what we need to understand in order to understand systematic and deep mutual misunderstanding, self-opacity, self-deceit, and other forms of limitation we are subject to when we try to learn what we need to know (but cannot) in cases of trust, love, and commitment.[17]

This is too telegraphic a statement of interpretive principles, and it gives no comfort to anyone convinced that the current modes of theory and the research enterprise are the best or even the only ones available, or to anyone who thinks that this approach is already ideologically biased, or to someone who complains that this is still professorial folderol about movies that are great and exciting fun, spoiled by "overinterpreting." The final point is easy enough to answer. It has been recognized for some time now that classic and contemporary Hollywood cinema is drastically undersold if there has to be some exclusive disjunction between either "commercial and entertaining" or "artistically ambitious." It is a mark of the geniuses of Hollywood cinema, Ford, Hawks, Sturges, Lubitsch, Ophüls, Welles, Lang, Cukor, Wilder, Hitchcock, and the like, that they found a way to achieve both.[18]

17.   So I disagree with Noël Carroll's understanding of the philosophical importance of *Vertigo*. He argues that because the philosophy at issue is "not for the graduate seminar room of a research university," it is philosophically revelatory, if it is, for its "target audience," "the general public." See Carroll, "*Vertigo* and the Pathologies of Romantic Love," in *Hitchcock and Philosophy: Dial M for Metaphysics*, ed. David Baggett and William A. Drumin (Chicago: Open Court, 2007), 113. A good deal of the film's philosophical revelation is certainly accessible to "the general public," but a very great deal more depends on multiple viewings, extremely close attention, and some awareness of the philosophical tradition. A very great deal is also simply very difficult to understand, apart from sustained and careful attention, of the sort we would not associate with "the general public," and much of it would indeed be a fit subject for a graduate research seminar, if the seminar were about the nature of the human struggle for mutual intelligibility.

18.   Correspondingly, in critical terms, if, in the current geography of the academic study of film, we can identify a common patch occupied by Stanley Cavell, Victor Perkins, Tom Gunning, Robin Wood, William Rothman, Murray Pomerance, George Wilson, Gilberto Perez, George Toles, and their like, I will be happy enough to find a home there. Not that anyone on this list would necessarily agree with any of what follows, or that I agree with all the positions they defend.

INTRODUCTION: THE ISSUE

It is sometimes said that in any romantic relationship between two people, six persons are involved.[19] There are the two persons they actually are; there are the two persons as they see themselves; and there are the two persons as they are each seen by the other. Once starting down such a road, though, it is hard to stop. One could say: there is also, for each, *the person they aspire to be seen as* by the other. This might be quite different from the person each actually is, and the person they see themselves as. That would get us to eight. If there is such a thing as self-deceit, there could be a difference between *the person they take themselves to be seen as* by the other and the *person they are really seen to be* by the other. And they might, in the usual mystery of self-deception, in some sense know this, and not be eager to correct the ideal perception. That would get us to ten. And if we import a Freudian thesis, the opposite-sex parent of each participant also would be involved, and that would get us to twelve — quite crowded, no matter the size of the drawing room or bedroom.

Something very like this complexity is necessary to understand the relation between Scottie and Madeleine, the two main players in Alfred Hitchcock's *Vertigo*. At the heart of the film is an immensely complicated, massively improbable and risky plot[20] by a San Francisco shipping magnate, Gavin Elster, to murder his wife, apparently because he has become bored with her shipbuilding business, and with life in San Francisco, where, Elster asserts, men used to have "power and freedom,"[21] but now do not.

19. It is said, for example, by Charles Barr, *Vertigo* (London: BFI Publishing, 2002), 57.

20. The film is *very loosely* based on a French novel, *D'entre les morts* (*From Among the Dead*), which was written specifically for Alfred Hitchcock by Pierre Boileau and Thomas Narcejac after they heard that he had tried to buy the rights to their previous novel, *Celle qui n'était plus* (*She Who Was No More*), which had been filmed as Clouzot's very fine *Diabolique* (1955). That title is likely an evocation of the quotation from the passage in Luke used as an epigraph to this book.

21. These same two words are repeated later in the film by Pop Leibel, the great authority on old San Francisco, who tells Scottie and Midge the story of Carlotta Valdez, and yet again by Scottie, when he is confronting Judy in the final scenes. A crucial feature of the new San Francisco, we find, is that what was once the public expression of male freedom and power has had to go underground, to disguise itself, but is still capable of success. It is also telling that what Elster uses to ensnare Scottie is a romantic mythology that, despite all the challenges to it by modern women like Midge, survives as powerful as ever.

He hires his old college friend, John "Scottie" Ferguson, a retired detective who left the force after a horrific accident.

In pursuit of a criminal with another policeman, Scottie had slipped on a rooftop, and while hanging on to a rain gutter, suspended many floors up, he froze in fright and vertigo, and could not extend his hand to the other policeman offering help. That policeman fell to his death while leaning farther over to grab Scottie, and so we learn that Scottie has acrophobia and gets vertigo in high places. Scottie quits the force, fearing his disability might cause another disaster.

Elster convinces Scottie that his wife believes herself to be, or is, haunted by a dead ancestor, Carlotta Valdez, and Elster wants Scottie to follow her around, to make sure this belief or haunting does not produce any harm to Madeleine. Elster's mistress, Judy Barton, is to impersonate Madeleine and seduce Scottie, lead him on until she gets him to an old Spanish mission, San Juan Bautista. This all succeeds. Scottie is deeply smitten, captivated by the erotic power of the melancholic Madeleine, even as he constantly tries to "disenchant" that mystery, explain everything in commonsense terms. Once at the mission, the fake Madeleine climbs to the top of a bell tower. As Elster knows, Scottie cannot follow because of his vertigo, so Elster can hurl the body of his already-dead wife off the tower, and Scottie is set up as the perfect witness to the supposed suicide.

Scottie suffers a nervous breakdown of some sort, and a year later, when he recovers, he wanders the city, "haunting" the places where he had followed Madeleine. In this wandering, he discovers a shopgirl with a striking, uncanny resemblance to Madeleine, Judy Barton. He becomes infatuated with her, and implores her to let him dress her, remake her, as Madeleine. The woman he has found, Judy, is in fact the former mistress of Elster hired to impersonate his wife, Madeleine, and it is only now, two-thirds of the way through the film, that the viewer learns, in a flashback of Judy's, the truth about the plot. Of course, when the transformation is finished, she *does* become "the woman Scottie loved," the fake Madeleine impersonated by Judy.

Scottie only suspects something when he sees a necklace that Carlotta had worn in a portrait, thus tying Judy to the earlier plot. Scottie drives her back to the mission and hauls her up the bell tower, finding in the process that he has overcome his vertigo, and in the midst of a complex, accusatory, and melancholic scene, Judy, surprised by a nun climbing the tower stairs, slips and falls to her death. For the third time in the film, a body falls by a helpless James Stewart. The film ends with Scottie poised on the ledge of the tower, overlooking the dead body of Judy/Madeleine.

So in the first part of the film, the Elster plot to murder his wife, since Scottie and Madeleine each are pretending to be someone else, we start out with at least four "selves." There is who Scottie really is (a retired detective) and who Madeleine really is (Judy Barton, Elster's mistress, enlisted to seduce Scottie so he could be used in the plot). Then there is the person Scottie is pretending to be (a casual wanderer, with no connection to Madeleine's husband, who just happens on Madeleine as she jumps in the bay), and who Judy is pretending to be (Elster's wife). As just noted, we might add the person whom Scottie takes Madeleine to be (he seems to buy the possession-by-ancestor fiction, or at least fears that it could lead to real suicide) and the person Madeleine takes Scottie to be (she knows he is not a casual wanderer and that he has been set up, but she understands herself to fall in love with "the real Scottie"). That is, they both know something about the other that they pretend not to know. One of the great complications raised by the film—as if this were not all complication enough—has to do with, given all this posing and false self-presentation, "*who* the woman is" whom Scottie falls in love with, and what consequences flow from the near impossibility of distinguishing real from apparent in this and perhaps many such important relationships.

Now unknowingness in various forms in general (from ignorance to being deceived, to fantasy thinking, to self-deceit) is something like a necessary condition of possibility of Hitchcock's cinematic world.[22] No other director is as adept and insightful in exploring cinematically what it is to live in, to endure, such a state of profound unknowingness, as well as depicting what great risks lie in store for anyone who challenges everyday complacency, the easy confidence that things are largely what they seem. That easy confidence itself, not acknowledging or appreciating the depth of this unknowingness, is also full of risks, chief of which is a moralism nar-

---

22.   I mean "world" here in the sense used by Stanley Cavell in *The World Viewed*, 20. Also indispensable on this topic: Victor Perkins, "Where Is the World? The Horizon of Events in Movie Fiction," in *Style and Meaning: Studies in the Detailed Analysis of Film*, ed. John Gobbs and Douglas Pye (Manchester: Manchester University Press, 2005), 16–41.

row enough to count as a kind of blindness. The list of his films in which the wrong person is blamed for or suspected of something, often confidently, smugly blamed, is very long,[23] and the primary technique used by Hitchcock to draw viewers into the film, to "co-experience" it, rather than merely observe it, *suspense*, is one built around either what we or characters know that others don't, or what we or other characters don't know but need badly to know in a dangerous situation. The suspense also often has a moral dimension: what we need to know but don't in order to resolve some moral question, or to warrant a dangerous decision to trust.[24] There are "shadows of doubt" everywhere in his films, doubts that have all sorts of implications for what the characters decide to do, and a kind of doubt that is not easy to eliminate.[25] In this film, the unknowingness theme has a specific inflection, a concentration on these multiple and shifting

23.   For example, most explicitly, *The Lodger* (1927), *Young and Innocent* (1937), *Saboteur* (1942), *The Thirty-Nine Steps* (1935), *Rebecca* (1940) (if you believe, as Fontaine's character does and most of us are led to believe, Maxim murdered his first wife, Rebecca), *Suspicion* (1941), *Spellbound* (1945), *Strangers on a Train* (1951), *I Confess* (1953), *The Wrong Man* (1956), *North by Northwest*; and there are others full of misplaced suspicion, confused identification, and wrongly directed moral censure. In *Stage Fright* (1950), the right person is blamed but the character we most identify with believes in his innocence, and throughout the film, so do we, convinced that the hypervamp, Marlene Dietrich, in one of her wonderful over-the-top villainess performances, must have done the deed. In *Blackmail* (1929) and *Sabotage* (1936), the right person is *not* blamed; two guilty women escape punishment (although there are extenuating circumstances for both). *Vertigo* is an ironic inversion: no one is accused, and *that* is the wrong.

24.   Recall Elster's plea: "Scottie, I need a friend, someone I can trust." On the "moral" dimensions of suspense, and its absorptive effect on viewers, see Robin Wood, "Why We Should Take Hitchcock Seriously," in *Focus on Hitchcock*, ed. Albert J. LaValley (Englewood Cliffs, NJ: Prentice Hall, 1972), 84–86. For a discussion of the general theme of trust as it is explored by noirs and noirish films like *Vertigo* and spy movies, see Robert von Hallberg, *"The Maltese Falcon" to "Body of Lies": Spies, Noirs, and Trust* (Albuquerque: University of New Mexico Press, 2015). The unusual moral tone of the film is something to be discussed later. I mean the absence of any grip of moral categories on the characters. Such notions never seem to arise, despite adultery and murder. The one that matters to Scottie is betrayal, although the sense in which it matters does not seem to be a moral one. As Wood points out aptly, when Scottie learns the truth, it would appear that for him, what initiates his rage and frustration is the only "crime" he is interested in: Judy's not being "his" Madeleine. Robin Wood, *Hitchcock's Films Revisited*, rev. ed. (New York: Columbia University Press, 2002), 386.

25.   In the 1943 film *Shadow of a Doubt*, the shadow refers to the doubt growing in niece Charlie's mind about her uncle Charles, which becomes a figure for her growing doubts about the adult world she is entering. She discovers both how difficult it is to resolve such doubts and how terrifying it may very well be to do so.

personae, a theme obviously also related to acting and film in general, with Hitchcock creating and deploying personae as actively as Elster and Scottie.[26] (In fact, in this film these multiple cinematic personae almost get out of hand. It is well known that Hitchcock wanted Vera Miles to play the role of Madeleine/Judy, but she became pregnant and couldn't accept. Nevertheless, it is reported that Hitchcock insisted that Novak play many of the scenes as he imagined Vera Miles would. So we have Kim Novak playing Vera Miles playing Judy Barton playing Madeleine Elster playing Carlotta Valdez.)[27]

I should note that I mean here, with this rather clumsy word, "unknowingness," to avoid suggesting that the problem is a kind of skepticism about interpreting others rightly, or skepticism about self-knowledge, or skepticism about the possible intimacies of romantic love. We don't know enough to be globally skeptical about these possibilities. There *are* occasions when we do get things right and we know that we do and have some sense of how we know, but not such that we could lay out evidence, or explain discursively how we know. But the fact that we understand something about ourselves and others that turns out to be correct is in itself of general significance. These moments of insight, though, cannot form the basis of a traditional philosophical rejection of skepticism, a counter-"theory" of the possibility of such knowledge. That there is no such theory is the basis for the illuminating and disclosive function of much art, both in being shown that there is no "solution" to such anxiety about our not knowing securely what we most need to know in our dealings with others and in exploring the lived-out implications of such a condition. In Hitchcock's representa-

---

26.   One of the many questions raised by this parallelism: Scottie re-creates Madeleine, a fictional Madeleine, who, it turns out, is the real Madeleine, herself a fiction. Therein may lie the truth of Hitchcock's fiction, the truth in fiction generally, in this case complicated by the suggestion that such a truth concerns the fictional nature of the self-representations that are the currency of our ordinary existence. This is a Proustian issue as well. See the fine discussion by Richard E. Goodkin, "Film and Fiction: Hitchcock's *Vertigo* and Proust's 'Vertigo,'" *MLN* 102, no. 5 (December 1987): 1171–81.

27.   Michael Wood provides a nice remark to sum up this condition: "In Hitchcock's films, it seems, there are only three options: to know too little, to know too much (however little that is), and to know a whole lot that is entirely plausible and completely wrong." Wood's remarks about Hitchcock's helping to provide us an "education in interpretation" are also very apt. Wood, *The Man Who Knew Too Much* (Oxford: New Harvest, 2015), x. It is also true that such unknowingness plays its more traditional, Shakespearian role in Hitchcock's comedies, like *The Trouble with Harry* (1955).

tion, we simply often (but not always) fail to know in situations where we most need to know, but we have no option but to persist in such attempts.[28] Not to persist would be not to lead a life at all. And there are intimations in many of his films of why this has become ever more difficult.

I also mean the term "unknowingness" to capture more than straightforward ignorance, such as ignorance about whether someone is being sincere, or what that person means to be doing by saying this or that to me now, in this context. The situations I am interested in are rarely cases of either complete knowledge or complete ignorance. We form various provisional views and see them partly confirmed, partly refuted; we are often uncertain whether what someone does confirms or refutes such a view. Often the unknowingness is convenient and we manage to "hide from ourselves" that we are in fact in the dark about someone. Often the "unknowingness" label does not properly capture the fact that we are in the dark because someone is keeping us in the dark. Being deceived, being self-deceived, being uncertain, but partly right, living over an extended period of time in a kind of suspension, having to make decisions about trust or disapproval, while uncertain of the relevant act descriptions or ascriptions of responsibility on which they are based, but not devoid of some markers of what would be the appropriate response, all amount to a swirl of uncertainty and partial confidence that, it seemed to me, required some capacious if unusual term. Hence "unknowingness." My hope is that its various inflections, and the demonstration that they are all inflections of a more general situation, can be made more concrete and compelling in what follows. (It is also not irrelevant, as the term "swirl" already indicates, that this situation is vertiginous, both for poor Scottie and the viewer.)

Further, this "Hitchcockian world" is a historical world, a complex modern world of profound social dependence and corresponding uncertainty, famously captured by Rousseau's remarks in the *Second Discourse* that modern "sociable man" lives "always outside himself, is capable of liv-

28.   I hope that my subtitle and these remarks manifest sufficiently the debt to Cavell's work in such an approach. For a fuller exploration of the unresolvable uncertainties in coming to understand and trust another, all of it inspired by Cavell's work, see Robert Pippin, "Passive and Active Skepticism in Nicholas Ray's *In a Lonely Place*," *nonsite.org*, no. 5 (Spring 2012), http://nonsite.org/article/passive-and-active-skepticism-in-nicholas-ray%e2%80%99s-in-a-lonely-place.

ing only in the opinions of others, and so to speak derives the sentiment of his own existence only from their judgment." This situation prompts the equally famous critique: "Forever asking others what we want, without ever daring to ask it of ourselves . . . we have nothing more than a deceiving and frivolous exterior."[29] We badly need to understand others to whom we are, because of this ever-greater division of labor and social dependence, vulnerable. We fear being misunderstood, or often we fear being truly understood, requiring the public and staged or partially staged personae so much a part of daily life. Rousseau seemed to think that simply being subject to such dependence produced the conformism and inauthenticity he saw emerging as a chief characteristic of modern societies, but it is just as much the case (and quite prominent in Hitchcock's films) that there is a reaction against such a state of social being that is just as tempting and the implications of which are just as pernicious: a false sense of, or assertion of, individual autonomy, a self-deceived insistence on self-sufficiency. We see this in Stewart's character in *Rear Window* (1954) and in Roger Thornhill, Cary Grant's character in *North by Northwest*, and it is quite prominent and important in the character Scottie in *Vertigo*.

Just what it is about the formation and structure of modern industrialized, bureaucratically managed societies that leads to an increasing likelihood of and anxiety about theatrical public personae is a vast and complicated topic. It takes in everything from the conditions of modern labor, the nature of the bourgeois family, the changing role of women, the influence of advertising and mass media, social media, and much else. But in a very general sense, some link between increasing social dependence (something that, for Rousseau, begins with the division of labor) and a growing fear of untrustworthy, theatricalized public personae, either in submission to this dependence or in self-deceived insistence on independence, is easy enough to see. We are *conscious* of this dependence and know that we must take some care, sometimes great care, about how we are perceived,

29.   Jean-Jacques Rousseau, *The First and Second Discourses Together with Replies to Critics and Essay on the Origin of Languages*, trans. Victor Gourevitch (New York: Harper and Row, 1986), 199. The later modern consequences of the situation Rousseau describes are nowhere illuminated better than in René Girard's *Deceit, Desire, and the Novel: Self and Other in Literary Structure* (Baltimore: Johns Hopkins University Press, 1961).

if we are to achieve any of our ends, and that we must depend on others, knowing that they are also taking such care. Since each of us knows this about the other, part of taking such care involves assessing the genuineness of the self-representations of others, such that aspects of our own self-representation will already reflect such an assessment. In ever-more-complicated networks of dependence, much of what we accept as fact, as reality, especially the large swath of reality that we cannot see or experience ourselves, is, unavoidably, a matter of testimony from others, others with whom we are sometimes in competition, and many others who, we know, have their own agendas and frailties. This is what gives us the endlessly complicated "world" of Laclos's *Les liaisons dangereuses*, Diderot's *Le neveu de Rameau*, chapter 4 of Hegel's *Phenomenology of Spirit* and its famous struggle for recognition between opposed self-consciousnesses, the novels of Henry James and Marcel Proust, and such critical works as René Girard's *Deceit, Desire, and the Novel*.[30]

One could say that Rousseau's and Hegel's revolutionary innovation in modern political thought was to identify kinds of *social* pathologies and wrongs beyond violations of rights and unequal material welfare. Issues like vanity, inauthenticity, psychologically damaging forms of dependence, manipulation in the guise of political dialogue, and harms that can occur in what Hegel summarized as that "struggle for recognition" were all to be treated as critical political issues. This is because such pathologies clearly can distort political will formation in democracies, can corrupt the public sphere in all sorts of ways, can degrade the credibility of the leaders of a re-

---

30. This theme of self-presentation and genuineness is a major one in *Notorious* (virtually nothing of how Alicia [Ingrid Bergman] and Devlin [Cary Grant] represent themselves to each other is true [the truth is that they care for each other; they represent themselves as contemptuous of each other, although neither knows that this is the case]). It is also prominent in *Spellbound* (the question of who John Ballantyne [Gregory Peck] is and how one might establish that is central) and in *Rear Window*, where for Jeff (James Stewart) and Lisa (Grace Kelly), the question of whether one can become "other" than who one is (war photographer, society woman) is a conversation staged for various ends each has, and left unresolved in the closing scene. (Lisa pretends to be preparing for her new life as a globe-trotter, but once Jeff falls asleep, she turns to her fashion magazine.) There are also many echoes (or instances of Hitchcockian "doubling") in *Marnie*, many pointed out by Wood, *Hitchcock's Films Revisited*, 173–97. Marnie's self-presentation is *wholly* theatrical, staged; but the narrative, while it culminates in a truth about the past, does not suggest that there is a "true" Marnie, after Mark succeeds in destroying the old one.

gime. (It would be a major digression into Rousseau to note how he thinks this issue bears on the dangers of theater in his *Letter to D'Alembert*,[31] especially since it would lead us to Hitchcock's concerns with the beholder's relation to fictional worlds in *Rear Window*. We have more than enough on our plate with the issue of unknowingnesss in intersubjective dynamics. But the problem of vanity gets a full and different sort of hearing in Rousseau's *Letter*.) Allegiance to a regime, especially up to the point of the "ultimate" sacrifice, is clearly not dependent on, or even much informed by, the best philosophical argument for the state's monopoly on legitimate violence. Understanding the wellsprings of such allegiance and what degrades it is a vital issue in political psychology, something that is not any longer a central topic in modern political theory or philosophy.[32] But it is an issue unto itself. In this context, what is relevant from this background is that the problems identified in the way summarized all inevitably raise an even more subtle, elusive, and more foundational issue. We could call it the *struggle for mutual interpretability*. I am suggesting that Hitchcock's greatest films are invaluable guides in coming to understand that problem, and, less directly, that the exploration of such issues in film and literature is philosophically indispensable, if we can frame and explore the issues in the right way. By "the right way," I mean, as noted earlier, doing justice to some level of general significance reached, without reverting to the level of abstraction necessary for philosophy as traditionally understood. *Shadow of a Doubt*, for example, is "about" a memorably unique sociopathic serial killer, but it does not aspire to treat Charles as an instance of a type, so that we might learn the psychological type. The film is obviously not "about" sociopaths. It is "about" such things as why Charles is able to hide so easily in Santa Rosa, about the costs to his niece Charlie in not only discovering who her beloved uncle really is, but in learning about the utter inadequacy of that town's (or, paradigmatically, her mother's) form of life for being able at all to take in who he is. So it is as much about American mores, and the brutality of the passage, when fully and truly undergone, from in-

---

31. Jean-Jacques Rousseau, *Letter to D'Alembert and Writings for the Theater* (Hanover, NH: University Press of New England, 2004).

32. For a fuller discussion of "political psychology," see Pippin, *Hollywood Westerns and American Myth*.

nocence to experience, a passage so difficult most of the characters in the movie have clearly never made it. That is the true "bond" between Charles and Charlie that is mentioned several times in the film.[33]

Of course, as Rousseau himself realized, such ever-more-complex interdependence is not avoidable in modern societies, but he was also concerned with more than the consequences of material dependence. In his *Confessions*, and *Nouvelle Heloïse*, and *Emile*, he also realized that our need for esteem in society, and the temptations to self-deceit it inspires, coupled with the possible self-doubts that arise from greater self-consciousness about these possibilities and temptations, has created a wholly new dynamic in history, one not present in ancient literature, Christian moral psychology, or medieval philosophy and theology, and one we do not (do not still) understand very well.

This complex of self- and other-representations is intertwined with another issue that bothered Rousseau—one's status as active and/or passive, subject or object (or the problem of "freedom and power" in the film's thrice-repeated refrain), in representing oneself, in being represented, and in trying to understand another's persona. If we accept this dependence in the wrong way, we live a life of endless compromises and conformism; if we try to ignore it or are indifferent to it, we risk egoism and a phony self-sufficiency. The latter seems to be Scottie's temptation; preferring to live alone, and even when facing death, hanging from the roof at the begin-

---

33.   I don't mean that Charlie comes to share her uncle's view that human life is a "foul sty," but she certainly has learned that what "Santa Rosa" thinks, by contrast, is a delusion. A few years earlier, in 1940, Hitchcock had been interested in the same issue in *Rebecca*. Joan Fontaine's character, the new Mrs. De Winter, is portrayed as "growing up" all at once in a long scene at the beach house with her new husband, Maxim (Laurence Olivier). It is a fine portrayal, as her posture, facial expressions, and voice change from the somewhat frightened ingenue, as she learns that her adored Maxim actually loathed his first wife, Rebecca, and is very likely guilty of some degree of manslaughter in her death, which Maxim covered up. This also, as in *Shadow*, raises questions about the moral implications of this transition. Fontaine's character, the new character, overjoyed that her husband has not been pining away for his ex, immediately and uncompromisingly pledges her help in covering up the deed. The fact that the first Rebecca was also dying of cancer seems to everyone, not least the authorities, to end all the speculation about how the boat suicide was supposed to have happened. This is similar to what happens to Nova Pilbeam's character (has there ever been such a fine actress name?) in *Young and Innocent* (aka *She Was Young*), although in this case the male lead is unquestionably innocent (as we discover; neither we nor she know this until the end).

ning, he cannot respond to the first words we hear, twice: "Give me your hand." But such a global assessment, stated this way, is too coarse-grained to capture the infinitely many interpersonal, psychological implications of life under conditions of such dependence, especially what is for many the foundation of modern social life, romantic love, assumed to be the heart of modern marriage and so the modern bourgeois family. For such explorations, we need imaginative geniuses like Alfred Hitchcock, and his cinematic account of this condition of unknowingness is my topic in what follows. (This hardly exhausts the philosophical significance of Hitchcock's films. Various and always futile attempts to escape from the past and to deny the fact of one's inevitable death, the inextricable "twinning" of good and evil, and the impossibility of pure "rightness" in a "wrong" world are also major themes, and all are important in *Vertigo*.)

For example: the natural companion film for this approach to *Vertigo*, with this sort of focus, would be *North by Northwest*, where a subject's "public" persona is fixed by accidentally being regarded as someone else, leading us to expect that the plot will concern how he returns to his "real self." But there are plenty of indications, starting with the fact that Thornhill is an advertising executive, that his "real persona" is a complex web of self-deceit, unknowing defensiveness, and a phony pretense of independence, which we are reminded of by the fact that he is disturbingly still very attached to his mother. The possibility that a person can be inhabited by another person, can even become another person, is of course prominent in *Psycho*. The question of "who" is present in the last scene is a link with many of the issues raised about *Vertigo* in this book. Hitchcock's "doubles" are also relevant, where we are asked to consider that two characters seem finally more like two sides of one character, as in the case of Bruno and Guy in *Strangers on a Train* and Charles and Charlie in *Shadow of a Doubt*.

This connection — between a certain kind of modern social world and the difficulties in self- and other-knowledge that Hitchcock explores — is not a frequent one in discussions of Hitchcock, but an emphasis on such a link is clear enough in many of his major films. As already mentioned, the general unknowingness of Santa Rosa, California, catastrophic in its implications, is quite a prominent, highlighted dimension of Charlie's quest for knowledge in *Shadow of a Doubt*. What is required of citizens, and especially the moral complexity of how they are to understand what is required of them, in a war or cold war situation, is emphasized in *Notorious*. The kind of desperation that life in an American small town can create, a desperation to leave, get out, at almost any price, and which is essential to understanding the motivation of Guy Haynes and his complex relation to his fiancée, is prominent in *Strangers on a Train*. In *Rear Window*, there is a famous angry speech, important in the film's treatment of a spectator-like relation to others, by a character whose dog has been killed, about the indifference, selfishness, and anomie of "neighborly life" in America. The prelude for Marion's theft in *Psycho* is a portrayal of the arrogance of those with money, the injustice of those with more than they know what to do with, and how that is felt by those without, and of the sexism and crass bullying the world of money and power seems to breed. The same emphasis on such ugliness is quite present in the businessmen from whom Marnie steals, and in their reaction, in *Marnie*. And, as noted, in *North by Northwest*, the film as a whole is framed as occurring in an America dominated by advertising, the creation and manipulation of appearances; that is, a world where there are no lies, as Roger Thornhill explains, just "expedient exaggerations." Even in *The Birds* (1963), after a major bird attack, there is a rant in the diner by a normal-looking woman, immediately hysterically xenophobic, convinced that the attacks must have something to do with the arrival of the "outsider," Melanie Daniels, Tippi Hedren's character.[34]

All these possibilities obviously involve a looser sense of personhood, and certainly a looser sense of personal identity, than is standard in philosophy. Let us say that we are dealing here with variations on the public personae persons might intentionally or semi-intentionally adopt. For our purposes, we can ignore the obvious relevance here of the work of Erving Goffman, "symbolic interactionism,"[35] performance theory, and so forth, and confine ourselves to what the film teaches us about how to watch it. These personae, how a person is trying to be perceived, are clear enough if we treat them as publicly presented self-representations.

34.   This characterization is one of many that could contribute to the claim that this struggle for mutuality, and its presupposition, mutual interpretability, becomes more and more difficult in modernity. Weber's notion of the increased differentiation of value spheres (church, family, class, ethnicity), many of which are incommensurable, and the corresponding absence of any shared ethical commonality, could also be invoked as ever-more-fragmenting aspects of modern civil society.

35.   I mean his famous book, *The Presentation of Self in Everyday Life* (New York: Anchor Books, 1959).

The putative distinctions and tension among these levels—"who I take myself to be," "who I am," and "the person you take me to be"—especially in intimate relations where each person matters a great deal to the other, often show up in conflict, misunderstanding, offense, wounded vanity, and attempts at setting things right. Moreover, every moderately psychologically aware person is also aware of the possibility of such discordance and can take that into account too. So there is some evolving, mutable, functional interdependence among my understanding of another, my understanding of his or her understanding of me, and my self-understanding, as well as mutable assumptions about what could or could not be possible, given the other and given the terms in which he or she matters to me. The relationship is dynamic, not static. What happens, what people do, is much more important than what people say, since the latter is never completely trustworthy, even if the speaker is sincere. So often our only means of determining what is real and what is theatrical is what we see, what we think we see, in what a person does, and *in a person's face*. (We usually don't get very far asking each other such questions as "What do you *really* think of me?" Or just by insisting, "I am *not* the person you take me to be." [Recall: "I am not a crook."])

So it is not for nothing then that the mysterious opening credits of *Vertigo* focus on a face, the face of some unknown woman, never shown in its entirely, only in a half close-up, and then in sections.[36]

1. THE OPENING CREDITS

She is not a character in the film (perhaps as unknown as Madeleine/Judy will forever remain), and her identity and role in the film are never returned to, never explained. Whoever this woman is, she simply appears, to a repetitive, mysterious, and suspenseful theme, the first of several powerful roles played by Bernard Herrmann's music throughout the film. It is

36. The theme of the "unknown woman" in all its senses is explored by William Rothman in "*Vertigo*: The Unknown Woman in Hitchcock," chap. 18 in *The Eye of the Camera: Essays in Film Criticism, History, and Aesthetics*, 2nd ed. (Cambridge: Cambridge University Press, 2004), 221–40.

clear enough that we are asked to think about the task of "reading a face" by having the stars' names literally appear in print "on" the face. (We are signaled about the level of difficulty this involves by never being shown the whole face, as if to say we are never actually given what we need to achieve any confident "reading." Everything will be and will remain tentative, partial, and so provisional.) "James Stewart" appears over the woman's mouth (figure 1), and this fits his role to come. He is an explainer and persuader, or at least he tries to be. He thinks he can explain Madeleine's strange feelings of being inhabited by Carlotta, and he clearly believes that by explaining them (apparently as some sort of confused actual memory, jumbled around in a fantasy world), he can exorcise the feelings and the fragmented memories. His words will do that. This is a feature of his false sense of self-sufficiency. He will even try to cure himself of vertigo, despite what the doctors say, by climbing kitchen stools and ladders to practice getting used to heights, as if he has understood his vertigo and can fix it. He fails.

Then we see "Kim Novak" at the bridge of the nose, just under the eyes, which shift somewhat nervously, perhaps guiltily, before the name appears (figure 2). We want to know, but are not shown, what the unknown woman sees. Us? What prompts the darting eyes, and so what are we seeing when we look at her? This all also touches on a familiar theme of Hitchcock's: the parallelism between the characters trying to "read" each other and what we

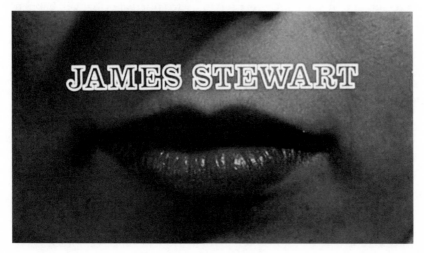

FIG. 1

FIG. 2

are doing in trying to read the film. (This is a theme given full treatment in *Rear Window*.) But a parallelism is not an identity. Nobody is more aware than Hitchcock that what we see on the screen are fictions made up by him and his team, designed to manipulate our reactions in various ways (as well as, if I am right, pose interpretive and philosophical questions). But he is also aware that he cannot have any desired effect unless his viewers are inspired to assess these fictional beings (they are fictional *human* beings, after all) and by such interpretation to try to anticipate what will happen, and reassess what they had believed when they learn something new.[37] Reading the film and reading its characters are intertwined. Thus the face on which the credits appear is itself treated as if it were a screen (in both senses of the word), the screen on which credits normally appear.

It is also appropriate that we look at someone *looking back at us* (appropriate, given what we will see in detail, that this self-other interpretive

37. The claim that so-called humanist readings of films confuse fictional screen characters with "real persons," or even that they encourage us to think of our relation to other human beings on the model of the unobserved observers, has always seemed to me to be based on several crude, simplistic, and tendentious misunderstandings of the relationship between these two things, however related they are in a limited way. Hitchcock himself, paradigmatically in *Rear Window*, not infrequently reminds us of this problem. For a longer discussion, see Robert Pippin, introduction to *Fatalism in American Film Noir*, 1–25.

FIG. 3

dynamic is an interchange, never merely observational), and interesting that the eyes briefly look away as we look at them (an avoidance of the direct gaze of another, perhaps in fear or embarrassment or suspicion), and that that the substance of the film seems to emerge from inside the eye (figure 3), foregrounding the problem of trying to know what is inside by looking at the outside, and emphasizing the connections between the meaning of the film, what is inside, or beyond what we see on the screen, and reading, trying to understand the meaning of, what we see on a face, the inside of what is outside. The colors change to a screen suffused with red, often the color of passion in the film (as green is the color of mystery, the unknown),[38] another nondiegetic moment that calls some brief

38.   "Green looms large in the film's color schemes, and is traditionally the color in which stage ghosts are bathed, presumably through association with green as the color of the fairies and therefore of the non-Christian supernatural in general." Raymond Durgnat, *The Strange Case of Alfred Hitchcock; Or, The Plain Man's Hitchcock* (Cambridge, MA: MIT Press, 1974), 294. Admittedly, this is a crude and introductory characterization of the role of color, a topic itself worthy of independent treatment. A very helpful such treatment: Eli Friedlander, "Being-in-(Techni)Color," in *Vertigo*, ed. Katalin Makkai (New York: Routledge, 2013), 174–93. Friedlander is certainly right that the colors are not strictly and uniformly "symbolic," nor are they mere indications of an accompanying, affective mood. In so far as they do express mood or tonality, they do so, he argues, as manifestations of mood, or *Stimmung* in the Heideggerian sense, disclosive of world itself (or what Heidegger would call the "worldhood of the world"), not as accompanying phenomena, indeed as a way of manifesting the to-

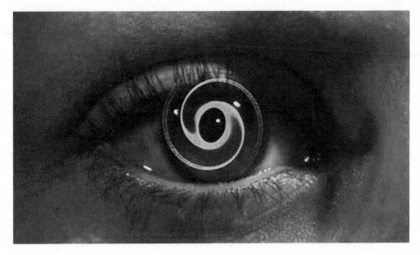

FIG. 4

attention to the narrator outside the film. And finally, it is appropriate that the dominant Saul Bass graphic symbols are spirals (figure 4), a circular motion around a fixed spot, like the obsession Scottie has with Madeleine, like the circular motion around the past that haunts him and eventually haunts Judy too, all connected to the vertiginous sensation of spinning.[39] (The "haunted Madeleine" ruse is also a spiral, with Madeleine revolving always around Carlotta; Madeleine is supposed to be the return, the re-incarnation, of her great-grandmother.)

So, if we are at all attentive in the first few seconds, we should be quite puzzled, since the question that we suggested above, one that could frame an attempt to understand the film at a more ambitious, philosophical level, immediately arises here. Why are we shown a close-up of half a face, and then led on what appears to be a specifically choreographed tour of

---

tality of that world. He also makes the fascinating point that these two colors are complementary, that staring at red and then looking at a light surface will produce an afterimage of green, and vice versa. While the colors do not constitute a "clear signifying system," as he argues, at least in an initial sense, this pairing suggests a link between erotic passion and the mysterious or even supernatural (not to mention with envy), and the way a whole world can be suffused with either.

39.   They are so-called Lissajous spirals and were animated for Bass by the young avant-garde film-maker and pioneer in computer animation John Whitney. For the details, see Dan Auiler, *"Vertigo": The Making of a Hitchcock Classic* (New York: St. Martin's, 1998), 153ff.

her mouth, nose, and eyes, on which the credits emerge? What is the point of opening the film this way? (One of the ironies of the scene is that, contrary to the usual results of a second or third viewing of the film, our return to this opening is even *more* puzzling, because we will have learned the woman shown is not a character in the film.)

We can at least say, though, that the puzzlement, or our not (actually, never) knowing "who this woman is," is itself significant, because it reminds us of a specific dimension of unknowingness throughout Hitchcock's great films. In his films we are constantly encountering people who are not who they say they are, creating the context that I am calling "unknowingness." Sometimes people are using aliases, like Marion Crane in *Psycho* and the title character in *Marnie*, or people simply pretend to be someone else, like Gregory Peck's character in *Spellbound* (because he cannot remember who he really is). And, of course, there is Judy pretending to be Madeleine Elster in *Vertigo*. In one case, in *North by Northwest*, a man pretends to be someone he believes exists, but who is fictional. Roger Thornhill is taken to be, then pretends to be, George Kaplan. (The Thornhill case is filled with more humor than most. We have a character who fits our description of Hitchcock's world. After the UN murder, he escapes and tries to hide "who he really is" from everyone. His glib, wise-cracking attitude is a manifestation of that attempt throughout. But when he is hiding his identity on a train, he thinks he succeeds by putting on a pathetically inadequate "disguise"—a pair of sunglasses, which does nothing to hide the distinctively gorgeous face "behind" the glasses. As Eve Kendall points out soon after they sit together, "It's a nice face.") More often, we encounter characters who are not the kind of person they pretend to be and are often taken to be in their community. Two paradigmatic cases of this are Norman Bates in *Psycho* and Uncle Charles, Joseph Cotten's character, in *Shadow of a Doubt*. But Alicia, Ingrid Bergman's character in *Notorious*, is not who she pretends to be, as part of infiltrating a neo-Nazi group, and, it turns out, is also not who all others (and probably the viewers, well into the film) take her to be, a promiscuous "tramp," with no principles. And Eve Kendall (Eva Marie Saint) is not who she pretends to be when she first meets Roger Thornhill in *North by Northwest*.

And in some cases, we see characters who do not intend to deceive or impersonate, but who are still not who they give others to believe they are, or who even turn out to be not the person or the kind of person *they* believe they are. They are unknowing in a specific sense; they are self-deceived. Guy Haynes (Farley Granger) in *Strangers on a Train* hides from himself how much his desire to marry the senator's daughter is tied to his desperate ambition to leave his small town and its tedium. (His willingness to do almost anything to free himself from his horrid wife may have given Bruno some reason to believe he would cooperate in the plot.) Jeff (James Stewart) in *Rear Window* has no access to his inability to establish any lasting commitments in his life. His self-representation to Lisa is sincere (as essentially, necessarily, a war and action photographer) but untrue. (No one is "necessarily" any one role in life.)[40] And in the paradigmatic case of such self-deceived unknowingness, we have Scottie in *Vertigo*, whose self-deceit is far too complicated to allow a telegraphic summary formulation. The anxieties and ironies of Hitchcockian unknowingness reach a kind of culmination in *Vertigo*, so it is perhaps appropriate that the film begins with a reference to a person who is never identified.

2. THE OPENING CHASE

The movie proper begins with a hand grasping a ladder railing and a person pulling himself up onto a roof, up from the depths to a great height, followed by a uniformed policeman, and then followed by a detective who, we learn soon afterward, is Scottie Ferguson. So we begin with another archetypal Hitchcockian theme, the pursuit or chase; and with its suggestion of a pursuer, the policeman, himself pursued (by Scottie), we get a foreshadowing of a familiar structure in Hitchcock's world. So, in *North by*

---

40.   He is self-deceived in a very familiar Sartrian sense, insisting he knows "essentially" who he is and must be, thus "fleeing" his freedom. It is typical of Hitchcock that he makes a very complicated point in a simple phrase or two. What Jeff does and is comfortable doing—photographing action and disaster scenes—requires only an eye for spectacle, whereas what Lisa wants him to be, a fashion photographer, requires an eye for what Jeff lacks and Lisa has, some psychological insight, an eye for how to see and then capture the inner in the outer. This might well also be a comment on what movies were becoming already in 1954, leaving behind Hitchcock's interest in psychological depths, and, accordingly, his interest in the clothes, look, and fashion of his films.

Northwest, Thornhill is pursuing the fictional Kaplan, but is himself pursued by the henchmen of Vandamm (James Mason), who are themselves pursued by an American spy service. This is another particular kind of unknowingness related to the active-passive theme. One thinks of oneself as pursuer, or something like the subject running the show, and is actually pursued, an object of pursuit. In *Vertigo*, at the beginning of the film, Scottie thinks he is pursuing, following, Madeleine, but he is actually being led by her, and "behind" it all is Elster.

When Scottie falls, and manages to hang on by grabbing a rain gutter, the policeman comes back for him and, on a very steeply inclined roof, quite selflessly tries to help Scottie by telling him, twice, "Grab my hand." It is not entirely clear how he could help Scottie, since his grip with his other hand hardly seems secure or firm. In fact, that hand seems to have no grip at all on the Spanish tiles of the roof. When Scottie looks down (plate 1), Hitchcock uses the zoom-forward-while-pulling-the-camera-back shot that he uses throughout the film to suggest Scottie's vertigo, caused, he learns for the first time, by a fear of heights, and in this case that seems to paralyze him. He freezes, and does not communicate with the policeman or try to extend his hand, and the policeman falls to his death.

I have already noted the significance of Scottie's inability to respond to this offer of help. As we will see, this first sign of his inability to acknowledge his dependence has something to do with his living alone, with his loneliness, with the less-than-intimate friendship he has with Midge, and ultimately with the enormous complexities of his relationship to Judy/Madeleine, especially when he assumes control of her remaking in the last third of the film. And many commentators have been puzzled by how desperate Scottie's situation is, even how inexplicable his finally being rescued must be. We have been shown no other policemen, and from what we are shown of the policeman's attempt to help, it is hard to imagine how anyone could get a secure enough grip on anything in time to save the rapidly weakening Scottie.[41]

But clearly the most important element introduced is the vertigo itself, especially since this beginning is one part of the major frame of the story.

---

41. Circumstances that have led Robin Wood to say of Scottie, "Metaphorically, he is suspended for the remainder of the film." Wood, *Hitchcock's Films Revisited*, 380.

It begins in life-threatening vertigo on a high building, and ends with Scottie "cured" of his vertigo, looking down from another height, the mission where Judy has slipped and fallen. Given our theme, the obvious question raised is whether he has learned, or come to understand something, has freed himself from the burden of unknowingness perhaps, and thereby no longer has the dizzying uncertainty of vertigo, assuming that could be one meaning of the ailment. And, of course, if so, what has he come to know? Obviously of crucial importance are what it means (beyond the simply pathological sense) that he has vertigo and what it means that he is cured, freed from it.[42] So is the general theme of heights and depths, a theme that touches on class and gender hierarchies, as we will see. Perhaps the most important note we can make about the vertigo is that one explanation of vertigo relevant to the film takes up the question, Any reasonable person would be nervous and cautious, even quite afraid, at great heights, so what accounts for the paralyzing and dizzying physical effects of the person who suffers from vertigo? A possible answer is that the unease stems from both a fear of falling and, at the same time, a fear of letting go, a fear of one's own attraction to death. So Scottie can be said to be suspended, as our dramatic first experience of him reveals, between both an attachment to and a melancholic detachment from his own life. Whether this turns out to be useful in understanding later episodes, and especially the ending, remains to be seen. It would also not be a stretch, if this diagnosis of vertigo is plausible, to connect that dynamic to something quite relevant to the alone and relatively aloof Scottie: the desire to fall in love, and the fear of falling in love.[43]

42. Later, in the first scene in Midge's apartment, she explains that the "doctors" think that Scottie can't be cured of his vertigo unless he has another "emotional shock," as if it doesn't matter what the content of the shock is. But it does seem to matter. In effect, he suffers another huge emotional shock, losing Madeleine again. The first time did not cure his vertigo (as far as he knows), but the second time, with him knowing that Madeleine is not, never was, Madeleine, but Judy Barton, he is cured.

43. Chris Marker has famously suggested that everything we see following the hospitalization is an insane man's imaginings. Marker, "A Free Replay (Notes on *Vertigo*)," in *Projections*, ed. John Boorman and Walter Donohue (London: Faber and Faber, 1995). Others have suggested that, given the obvious impossibility of any credible account of how Scottie could have been saved from his position hanging from the building in the first scenes, the entire movie is what he imagines as he falls to earth. This would be a variation of Ambrose Bierce's story "An Occurrence at Owl Creek Bridge." See James F. Maxfield, "A Dreamer and His Dream: Another Way of Looking at Hitchcock's *Vertigo*," *Film Criticism* 14, no. 3 (Spring 1990): 3; and Barr, *Vertigo*, 32.

But the term "vertigo" is multiply determined and its role in the film could sustain several complementary interpretive directions. The sheer density of interpretive possibilities, for the characters and for us, is also vertiginous, as is the state of unknowingness itself, as is the anxiety that one might not be oneself, might be "haunted," with all the metaphorical possibilities that implies, by another person or an older version of oneself, a "ghost" that keeps recurring even though one thinks it has been left behind, exorcised.

3. INTRODUCING MIDGE

The mise-en-scène shifts dramatically in the first scene after the chase and fall, from darkness and danger to a bright, sunny, very cluttered apartment (plate 2), with a panoramic view of San Francisco (the apartment is on Telegraph Hill, overlooking Russian Hill) out of a large window. A vast amount of thematic and cinematic material is densely packed into this opening in the apartment of Scottie's friend, Midge, and it repays close attention. A petite blonde woman in a yellow sweater who, we learn, is a longtime friend of Scottie's from their college days and beyond, Midge (a commercial artist working on advertising for ladies' underwear),[44] is drawing at a drafting table. She stays seated for most of the scene, drawing while she and Scottie talk. (Later we learn that John Ferguson is "Scottie" to most of his associates and "John" or "Johnny" to his "close friends." In the film Midge is the only one who calls him "Johnny" or "Johnny-O," but since everyone else calls him "Scottie," I will follow that convention except when speaking from Midge's point of view. It is of course significant that he has several names, and that Madeleine/Judy calls him "Scottie.") James Stewart, in a brown suit, is trying to balance a cane on his finger. Some classical music (it is J. C. Bach)[45] is playing softly in the background. He is

44. This is not entirely clear. From the sketches we see, she may be designing underwear. But since she is working on an already-designed brassiere, I assume she must be drawing advertising copy.
45. The clarity and "rationality" of the music of any Bach, or Mozart, is shut off as a kind of sign that the clarity, balance, order, and general sense made in this type of music will not be appropriate

not very good at the balancing; the cane falls and he cries out in pain, re-enacting in a strange, comic way the fall and scream we have just heard. He can't "balance" (so we are also reminded of his general vertigo problem, and so what his "lack of balance" might mean in some larger sense). The pain is caused by his injury, and he is wearing a back brace while recuperating. The shift to the apartment is abrupt not only because of the striking contrast between night and day, outside and inside, danger and peacefulness, but because the tone of the conversation and the action is now quite lighthearted, jovial, even though we soon learn that Scottie, a man who looks to be in his late forties or early fifties (Stewart was forty-nine in 1957), has just ended the only career he has ever known (he resigned from the force, worried that his vertigo could return at a crucial moment, an ominous foreshadowing since it will), and we learn that in his sleep he often sees the falling policeman and reexperiences his inability to accept his help, although he speeds right by that issue. We sense, vaguely to be sure, some sort of dissociation.

There are also clear references to *Rear Window*, made four years earlier, also starring James Stewart.[46] The Stewart character is unmarried again, and in both cases not just by chance but because of some reluctance, because of some failure to connect with others, figured by their immobility. He is not as immobilized as he was as Jeff in *Rear Window*, where he had a whole leg in a cast,[47] but he is in what he refers to as a "corset" (he does not call it a "back brace" or "back support") that restricts his freedom of movement, and these immobilizings in both films seem to figure for us some psychological constriction. Both movies begin with conversations about getting free of what is immobilizing Stewart's character, which, in both cases, is internal. The same problems caused by both the cast and the corset are noted, especially, in both openings, the inability to "scratch where it

to the depths into which we are about to descend—all a prelude to making this explicit: "I don't think Mozart is going to help." For this move and these events, only something Wagnerian will do.

46.   Gregg M. Horowitz provides an illuminating discussion of the many links and also dissonances between *Rear Window* and *Vertigo* in "A Made-to-Order Witness: Women's Knowledge in *Vertigo*," in Makkai, *Vertigo*, 112–38.

47.   At the end of the film, he ends up with both legs in a cast, suggesting that his immobility, and all that it means, has not been solved, but actually worsened, despite what appears to be a "happy ending" and a newly found appreciation for his girlfriend Lisa (Grace Kelly). As noted, that reconciliation is clearly presented as an illusion.

itches," perhaps also a limitation of some more general significance. So the "twinning" of Jeff and Scottie foregrounds the problem of this constriction or limitation, all in a way, I think it is fair to say, we the viewers are being asked to consider.[48]

But the conversation takes a distinctly different, curious turn in *Vertigo*, signaled already by Scottie's use of "corset," the feminine undergarment, for what he is wearing. Some aspect of his powerlessness seems to him, it would appear, feminizing. (This is important for later. For the first time in his life, Scottie has lost his job, his identity, is suddenly cut off from everything he recognized as his life, is now left only to "wander." It would be understandable if he feels somewhat emasculated, a man in a corset with nothing to do, and vulnerable. It is just this vulnerability that Elster will exploit.)[49] Or at least, that (that he is no longer a man) is what he clearly fears. For he abruptly asks Midge, with a look of real consternation or even anxiety on his face, without irony, whether many men wear corsets. "More than you would think," she replies, as if to suggest a large number of men going about in female undergarments, probably worried about being discovered. (This all goes on as he keeps handling, fondling one might even say, that phallic cane of his [figure 5].)

Bu the conversation gets odder. Scottie asks if she knows this about male corsets "from personal experience." Remarkably, he is asking her if she knows this fact by having slept with men who wear corsets. It is a kind of adolescent, jokey remark, and Midge responds in a way that will be explicitly thematized very soon, and then once more in the apartment, and then one final time, after the fake suicide. She gives him an unamused, *motherly*, drawn-out "pleeease" and turns the conversation to something much more adult. She asks why he is retiring and what he will do in retirement. He tells her, still joking (and evading the seriousness of the issue), that he might get dizzy sitting at a desk, and this makes her laugh, saying "Oh, Johnny-O"

48.   Another connection between the two is the relation between Midge and Stella, Thelma Ritter's character in *Rear Window*, also a wise, sensible, but thoroughly unerotic, professedly unerotic character. (Cf. her little speech on companionate marriage.) As Fred Rush has pointed out to me, Hitchcock goes so far as to emphasize the physical contact between Jeff and Stella (massage) as completely devoid of any erotic connotation. (And yes, one could say that, with respect to the disappearance of eros when the "sensible" considerations are paramount, Hitchcock wants to "rub it in.")

49.   See the discussion in Susan S. Levine, "Means and Ends in Hitchcock's *Vertigo*, or Kant You See?," *International Journal of Psychoanalysis* 96 (2015): 225–37, esp. 227–29.

FIG. 5

with a bemused look on her face, exactly as a mother might say to a favored son who can always make her laugh. He says he will do nothing, that he is a man of fairly independent means. We are introduced for the first time to the theme of "wandering," which will reappear several more times, as well as the theme of independence. When she asks if he wouldn't like to take a trip, he explicitly chastises her for acting "motherly," and she gives a slight indication, a pause and a look, that she is wounded by the term, although she continues in the tone of a patient mother and he in the tone of a jocular boy. This also touches on a theme of great importance to Hitchcock, the role of mothers in modern domestic life, all the way from portraying them as tyrannical, smothering, needy, and unsympathetic in films like *Notorious*, *Psycho*, *The Birds*, and *North by Northwest*, to portraying them as what appear to be paragons of the stereotypical maternal role, as in *Shadow of a Doubt* and both versions of *The Man Who Knew Too Much* (1934, remade in 1956), but who are clearly chafing under such severe restrictions, and desperately searching for some escape. This seems to have something to do with Hitchcock's interest in psychoanalysis and the Oedipal problem and his sense of the unusually strong role played by mothers in American domestic life in particular.[50]

50.   See the interesting discussion by Elsie B. Michie, "Unveiling Maternal Desire: Hitchcock and American Domesticity," in *Hitchcock's America*, ed. Jonathan Freedman and Richard Millington (Ox-

FIG. 6

And this dimension becomes even more explicit in an even more unusual twist in the conversation. Scottie looks at a model brassiere she is also drawing and asks what it is, and she replies, returning to the "motherly" theme, that it is a brassiere, that he knows about such things, he is a "big boy, now." But the brassiere has no shoulder straps and no back straps; "revolutionary uplift," Midge says. She explains that it is based on a cantilevered bridge; an aircraft engineer designed it in his spare time (figure 6). No doubt, we are being introduced to the notion of something exterior, clothing, or an appearance that is some sort of illusion, not what it seems. It could also be a bit of foreshadowing, since the first time we see Madeleine, in quite a powerful evocation of the film noir convention of our first look at the femme fatale (and the stunned reaction and immediate submission of the noir protagonist), she might be wearing something like the cantilevered bra.[51] We see her first from the rear, her exposed back in a black evening dress with a green wrap, and the back is strapless.

This is a long way around the barn to make a point about Midge's

ford: Oxford University Press, 1999), 29–54. The theme may also have something to do with the strong role his wife, Alma, played in the making of the majority of his films.

51.   The links between *Vertigo* and film noir conventions, especially about women, are discussed by James Harvey, *Movie Love in the Fifties* (Cambridge, MA: Da Capo, 2005), 28–42, and by Homer B. Petty, "Hitchcock, Class, and Noir," in *The Cambridge Companion to Alfred Hitchcock*, ed. Jonathan Freedman (Cambridge: Cambridge University Press, 2015), 76–91.

role—actually two points. The first is that her relationship with Scottie is more motherly than erotic, an issue that will come up again when they discuss their past. Their relation to female undergarments has no tinge of eros about it, either in memory or in any prospect. The second is the principle of the cantilever—to keep something up, *to prevent it from falling, without visible support.* Or at least, Midge's constant support for him seems invisible to Scottie. That is the role Midge has apparently assumed in Scottie's life.[52] He walks into her apartment frequently, without knocking, comes over to discuss the latest events of the day. They have dinner and go to films together, but there is so little romantic spark between them that their relationship resembles nothing so much as a close, long-time friendship between a woman and a gay man, or friendly siblings, or a devoted mother-son pairing.

That (a complete lack of anything erotic between them) is not wholly true, of course, as the next strange turn in the conversation makes clear. Scottie abruptly asks, "How's your love life?" presumably the 1950s version of "Are you having sex with anyone?" She replies that her love life is "normal" after noting, "That's following a train of thought" (from bras to love life). Throughout all of this, and the unusually tense conversation that follows (not that Scottie notices the tension at all), she continues to sketch the new brassiere, speaking in the same calm, moderate tone she uses throughout, her voice only occasionally inflected with a slight irony. Scottie asks her a cruel, almost taunting question (clearly, however, without knowing, or allowing himself to acknowledge, that that is what he is doing): "Aren't you ever gonna get married?" She responds as he and she obviously know she will, that there is only one man in the world for her. The question touches on what are clearly familiar and painful issues. And he notes that she means him, and then, increasing the cruelty of the question, he pretends to have trouble remembering whether they were ever engaged: "We were engaged once, weren't we?" Who forgets whether they were ever engaged? A tiny visual detail gives away the insensitivity of the question and the depths of feeling that are behind her measured response. Hitchcock switches to a tight close-up, and we see her eyes raised

52. It may all also be a Hollywood in-joke, since there is a well-known rumor/story that Howard Hughes had an engineer design a new underwire bra for Jane Russell.

in a knowing and pained gesture, a forced tiny smile on her face, as if she knows both that he is taunting her (thinking he is being playful) and that he does not know how cruel he is being (plate 3). "Three whole weeks," she says. He reminds her that she was the one who called it off (although we sense, mostly by her discomfort, that this is quite a simplistic characterization), and he says that he is still "available," making the unintentionally ironic point that he was not and is not now at all available. We see another close-up of Midge, another pained look (but not so pained that he would notice), but now with no hint of a smile, and a sudden look of genuine distress (plate 4).

Scottie asks if she remembers Gavin Elster from college; he wants to see Scottie. She does not. They both think that the address is a skid row address and that Elster is on the bum and wants to hit him up for a drink. Scottie remarks that he too is now "on the bum," although he clearly has ample means, and if Elster were living on skid row, it would be (in a way typical of Scottie, we will come to see) insensitive to pretend otherwise, to pretend that they are in similar circumstances. The heights of money and power, Elster's actual position, are here confused with the "down and out" by an outward sign, the address, the kind of sign we all use to make these snap judgments.

The scene closes with a manifestation of Scottie's view of his presumed rational control over his situation. (It is instructive that earlier he had some vague sense of the insufficiency of his presumed "independence." He says that he is a man of independent means, and then immediately qualifies that with "fairly independent.") In reaction to Midge reporting that the doctors think his situation is not curable apart from another "emotional shock," and even that wouldn't probably cure him, he insists, "I think I can lick it," and proposes that he can very gradually get used to heights and overcome his vertigo. (An early manifestation, perhaps, of behavioral or cognitive therapy.) This proves, predictably, untrue. As he steps to the top of a step ladder, he looks down and sees out the window. He is at a greater height than he supposed, and he has underestimated not only the height but his vulnerability to vertigo, and faints. It would probably be more accurate to say he swoons, plays out what would be the stereotypical role of the fainting woman, as the theme of femininity, being mothered, a fear of impotence (or perhaps castration) raised by his anxiety about his corset and the discussion of female undergarments, and his inability to respond to the policeman, is given a visual inflection. He falls into her arms, and the apartment scene closes with her uttering a plaintive, pitying, motherly "Oh, Johnny" (plate 5). (Foreboding plays an important role in the film, a cinematic element that often suggests that a character's fate is already sealed, that there is little he or she can do to avoid what is going to happen to him or her. The present is already filled with the future. The flowers that Scottie sees, in the left corner of the window as he looks down, are very similar to the kind of flowers he will soon see Madeleine buy, the flowers that Carlotta is holding in the portrait of her.)[53]

This scene establishes a number of premises for the action to follow. There are two that should be highlighted. First, we have seen that Scottie's confident, breezy air and his assumption of an "old pals, buddies" friendship with Midge reveal a marked failure to understand the practical effect what he says has on Midge. He does not register any of her pained expressions or her muted responsiveness when he discusses their engagement, does not seem to have the ability even to imagine what it would be for her to go through this conversation with him. In a word, Scottie is a bit dense psychologically: unknowing about himself, his vertigo, what is going on beneath the surface with Midge, his own vulnerability and anxieties. A "big boy," but still in many ways a boy. So the scene is our introduction to an instance of a failure of mutual interpretability, since it is also clear that, while Midge wants to help, she also does not seem to appreciate what her adopting such a motherly role could mean for Scottie, has no sense that it may be infantilizing, perhaps even emasculating. So their failure to understand each other very well seems linked with the limited self-understanding each possesses. Their ability, in the dynamic that unfolds, to interpret what the other "really" means to say or do will be put to a severe test and they will both fail badly. As we will see, Midge's attempt to use "music therapy" to cure Scottie of his near catatonic depression after the fake suicide of Madeleine is on a par with Scottie's attempt to "cure himself" of vertigo: a pathetic, deluded assertion of control over elements Hitchcock regularly

<hr>

53. Another way for Hitchcock to suggest the underlying tension and misunderstanding keeping them apart is purely cinematic. The apartment discussion consists of sixty-two shots, in only five of which are Midge and Scottie in the same frame. See Wood, *Hitchcock's Films Revisited*, 381.

treats as not controllable. In fact, that later scene is carefully set up by what most viewers would not notice on a first viewing, that Hitchcock makes a point of having Scottie, in this apartment scene, object to the classical music in the background. He clearly is no fan; it even irritates him, is "giving him vertigo right now." And just as clearly, this has not registered on Midge. Later, when Scottie is hospitalized and sunk into a kind of catatonia, she brings along the very type of music, classical music, Mozart, that he had objected to. (In the apartment, she responds so quickly to his request to turn it off that we get the sense that this has been a running issue between them for years. No matter—she brings along her Mozart anyway, perhaps in the way a mother would claim to know "what is best" despite her son's protestations.) This is a small, almost incidental marker for an important point, her inability to understand Scottie, and it is typical of the way Hitchcock structures his films so as to require multiple viewings.

The other important element introduced is simply the character of Midge herself, and Scottie's relation with the somewhat dowdy, mothering, sane, practical Midge we are introduced to. Her very name and, in a movie about heights, her stature tell us a great deal. In the dynamic that develops, Midge's diminutive stature, her weak psychological presence in the drama, and so her inability to light any romantic spark in Scottie are products of her unknowingness. Put simply, being so attentive to Johnny in her motherly way, she is also thereby indirectly submissive to him, so submissive to his needs that she cannot properly "see" him or be seen by him, wants only to be seen by him on whatever terms he requires, wants to be married to him, "whoever" he is. The height (no pun) of her misunderstanding of Johnny occurs later, when she literally tries to paint herself into his sight, his regard, by painting her face on Carlotta's body in the portrait Madeleine visits.[54] But *to be seen* as she wants to be, she must also *rightly see*, something she can't do.[55]

On the other hand, someone has to be the grown-up in this group, and

54. Midge wants to enter Scottie's fantasy, but only to debunk it. There is thus a parallel with Judy trying hard to *keep* Scottie from entering that fantasy again. Judy though, rather than being limited to Midge's artificial devices, can literally become the fantasy again, clearly hoping that in some way by entering it, she can lead Scottie out of it. Cf. Wood's remarks, *Hitchcock's Films Revisited*, 126.

55. In Durgnat's apt phrase, "better Scottie dissatisfied than Midge satisfied." Durgnat, *The Strange Case of Alfred Hitchcock*, 287.

it is testimony to the film's ability to evoke the power (and the potential destructiveness) of romantic fantasy that the viewer can get so caught up in it that Midge seems dull or pedestrian, unworthy of Scottie's attention. That would be a mistake. She is simply a mature, reasonable woman in love with a man who will only accept her regard in a very limited way, a way she somewhat grudgingly accepts rather than have no friendship at all. In this, she is playing out a familiar film noir role in a frequent romantic triangle in that genre (the closest genre to *Vertigo*), among a man, a mysterious, alluring, but untrustworthy femme fatale, and her rival, a "normal" or "domestic" woman without the aura and allure of the femme fatale, but infinitely more dependable. Perhaps the classic case is the triangle in Jacques Tourneur's *Out of the Past* (1947). This structure is repeated in Charles Vidor's *Gilda* (1946), and André de Toth's *Pitfall* (1948), but there are endless variations, such as Fritz Lang's *Scarlett Street* (1945), where the "domestic" woman, the wife, is unbearable, and it is present in many other genres, most famously, Michael Curtiz's *Casablanca* (1942) (with genders reversed), and it is a staple of many westerns, like *Shane* (1953) and *High Noon* (1952) and *The Man Who Shot Liberty Valance* (1962), where the choice is either a woman's, between a charismatic and sexy gunfighter or ex-gunfighter and a "town" or "farm" man, or a man's, between a barroom girl and a wifely sort.[56] The structure is also clearly invoked in *Marnie*. But for our purposes, it introduces us, by a kind of preliminary contrast, to the "other" of Midge, Madeleine, and so to the potentially irrational and destructive attractions of fantasy in romantic love, not, perhaps, as an occasional pathological by-product of such love, but essential to its possibility.[57] But first, we need to meet the villain in the drama, Gavin Elster.

---

56. The frequency of this structure, its mythic structuring of plot, certainly warrants further treatment. See, for example, Robert B. Ray, *A Certain Tendency of the Hollywood Cinema, 1930–1980* (Princeton, NJ: Princeton University Press, 1985).

57. By "irrational" I don't mean strategically irrational. I mean cases when we cannot give ourselves good reasons, even relativized to our particular interests, for what we are doing, and even realize that there are several good reasons, in all senses, for not doing what we are doing. Moreover, I mean this to be a *question* raised by the film, not an assertion. Scottie's obsession with Madeleine is hardly a paradigmatic case of a "Romeo and Juliet" kind of romantic love. The question is whether it highlights elements of romantic love that we would often like to disregard, such as the role of fantasy and the high level of unknowingness we are quite capable of tolerating.

4. GAVIN ELSTER AND THE SCHEME

The address Scottie has turns out to be Elster's office at his ship-building yard, and it is far from down and out. It is large, luxurious, and furnished in a way that constantly calls to mind old San Francisco, especially the many photographs and paintings on the wall (figure 7).

But before the conversation begins, Hitchcock makes his by now obligatory cameo appearance, strolling past the office, carrying a small musical case, perhaps a French horn (figure 8). The question of the purpose of these cameos, aside from commercially building his brand, which is undoubtedly part of it, is an independent topic that would take us far afield. But in this case, I cannot resist noting that he is having a bit of fun. The stroll is a reference to his cameo in *Strangers on a Train* (figure 9), also carrying a musical instrument, but in that case, one shaped very much like him, and he is enormous, much heavier than seven years later. (He looks like he was easily at the three hundred pounds he topped off at when making *Foreign Correspondent* [1940].) He seems to have slimmed down a good deal in the years since *Strangers*, and his tiny musical case, and his profile shot, proudly make his point.

The Elster office scene is much like the apartment scene. On a first

FIG. 7

FIG. 8

FIG. 9

viewing, it would appear to be simple scene setting and small talk. As in the apartment scene, we are just carried along, absorbing background and plot details as they whiz past us. That is, by and large, in the apartment we do not immediately notice how poorly Scottie and Midge are understanding each other, and do not notice much the hostility of Scottie for Midge about her "mothering," or his aggressiveness in pretending not to recall whether they were engaged once, or perhaps even her discomfort. (The implicit suggestion in a lot of Hitchcock's work is that we could film almost any conversation among intimates, and, *if it is filmed intelligently*, we could be brought to see a dynamic that none of the participants seem to notice. This is connected with Hitchcock's interest in Freud and psychoanalytic explanation, but is not limited to that form of unknowingness alone, the unconscious. Vanity, erotic passion, need, self-deceit, and various social hierarchies, like class and gender, are all among the factors that play out in impeding any secure self- and other-knowledge.)[58] In the office scene, we do not at first notice much that Elster yearns for an older San Francisco, one represented by a painting Scottie is looking at; or note that what Elster means is the San Francisco of "color, excitement," and especially "the power, freedom." We cannot know from this scene that he is talking about the exclusively rich, white male power and freedom that allowed a wealthy man to take a young Mexican concubine and, when tired of her, take their child and "throw her [the mistress] away." (Another hierarchy that brutally closes off any possible mutuality is the colonization of the West and the imperial power that is the source of the Carlotta story.) The phrase "power and freedom" occurs twice more. In Pop Leibel's bookstore as he tells the original Carlotta story, and it is uttered by Scottie near the end, when he is demanding the truth from Madeleine. He remarks on all that "power and freedom" Elster had, the power and freedom, at least in this version of the film, the final version, that allowed this wealthy man to get

58.   This is not to deny that a great deal of *Vertigo* lends itself to psychoanalytic explanation, or to deny that Hitchcock intended to suggest such explicability. Especially relevant to this film, for one of many possible examples, would be Freud's 1910 essay, "A Special Type of Choice of Object Made by Men," in *The Standard Edition of the Complete Psychological Works of Sigmund Freud*, vol. 11, *Five Lectures on Psycho-Analysis, Leonardo da Vinci and Other Works (1910)*, trans. James Strachey (London: Hogarth, 1994), 163–76. This has to be qualified though, and I try do so below.

away with murdering his wife and living off her wealth.[59] (What Scottie does not notice later is that he too is exercising a power and freedom, one granted him by Judy, to remake the world as he wants it, indifferent to anything about Judy other than how she can be made to look, made to look for him, a figure for the more general fate of women in the world depicted by *Vertigo*.)[60]

We also do not know yet that Hitchcock will present us with several ways of understanding the bearing of the past on the present. Some people, like Judy, will want to escape from what they did in the past, work to forget and ignore it. In the fantasy of Carlotta, the past inhabits and threatens to take over the present, a figure for the inescapable burden of past colonialism that Hitchcock drops lightly into the film. And for some, like Elster, the past represents the utopia of white, male power, and he is willing to murder to have a taste of it.

The dialogue in the office involves quite an elaborate choreography of movement: standing, sitting, and positions "above" (there is a raised floor in one section) and "below."[61] For the most part, Elster is representing himself as at his wit's end, dependent on Scottie for help. As happens frequently, especially to Scottie, someone who thinks he is the subject, running the show, with others dependent on him, is in reality the object

59.   Nervous for a while about European distribution, Hitchcock filmed a scene after the bell tower finale in which Scottie returns late at night to Midge's apartment, after she has heard on the radio that Elster has been apprehended and is being extradited. It can be seen in the "Special Features" section of the Blu-ray version of *Vertigo* (Universal Home Entertainment, release date May 6, 2014) as "Foreign Censorship Ending."

60.   The general commodification of beauty in consumer societies is not unrelated to the status of the ideal of the beautiful in modernity, including what had been assumed to be its moral power from Plato to Kant and Schiller. See Robert Pippin, "*Vertigo*: A Response to Tom Gunning," in *Erotikon: Essays on Eros, Ancient and Modern*, ed. Shadi Bartsch and Thomas Bartscherer (Chicago: University of Chicago Press, 2005), 278–81. I discuss there some of the Proustian themes touched on by Goodkin, "Film and Fiction," most importantly the attempt by Scottie to deny the most fundamental aspect of human finitude, its temporality, the utter pastness of the past. Goodkin has some valuable things to say about the relation of this theme to fiction, and the relation between fiction and cinema.

61.   There is a very valuable, detailed analysis of the way the blocking of the scene works: Bryan Menegus, "The Hidden Trick in Almost Every Classic Hitchcock Scene," *Sploid* (blog), March 23, 2016, http://sploid.gizmodo.com/the-hidden-trick-in-almost-every-classic-hitchcock-scen-1766617503. See also Wood, *Hitchcock's Films Revisited*, 383.

FIG. 10

of someone else's manipulation, and in general the complex positioning can be seen as playing out visually the assumptions by each of the inter-locutors about his relative position in respect to the other (plate 6 and figure 10).

It is when Elster is at his most deceptive and manipulating, however, that the pretense of mutuality is at its most visible. He meets Scottie face-to-face, both standing, and tells him that he needs a friend, someone he can trust. In one sense, this is a hard request to turn down, but in another, it is not prudent to get so involved with someone Scottie has not seen in some thirty years, someone whose name Midge does not even recognize (figure 11).

We will discover soon that it is precisely the more outlandish elements of the story Elster has told him, a mysterious possession by a dead woman, that most captivate Scottie, even though he expresses something close to contempt when Elster asks him if he believes in such things. And Elster clearly has no worries resting Scottie's decision not on their presumed friendship but on what will happen to Scottie when he first sees Made-leine. He seems completely confident that her beauty and allure will in-stantly overcome any hesitation. His plan succeeds well beyond anything he could have imagined.

FIG. 11

5. ERNIE'S

This idea of the irrational[62] power of beauty and sexual allure—that is, Elster's supreme confidence that just *seeing* Madeleine, all by itself, will overcome any hesitation Scottie has—is on a par with, as fantastical as, the
notion that a dead woman could haunt a living woman, although the former is much more commonly accepted than the latter. It will become clear
very soon in the film that Scottie is as "haunted" by Madeleine (or, we
have to say, his fantasy Madeleine, since he never really learns very much
about her) as Madeleine pretends to be by Carlotta. (With one obvious
exception: Judy/Madeleine is only pretending to be haunted and driven
to suicide. Scottie is genuinely "haunted" or under a spell, as Judy will be
genuinely "haunted" later by her own past pretense of being Madeleine.)
Both hauntings introduce us to the world of fantasy, projection, obsession,
being "stalked" by the past, erotic "spells," and the like.

However unusual, though, Elster is certainly right. One look, and it
might even be one look at Madeleine's *back*, is all it takes for Scottie to "fall."

---

62.   Again, I mean by this a situation in which one finds oneself doing something for which one
can give no good reason. A paradigmatic case in the film occurs later when Judy asks Scottie why he
is doing this, remaking her, and he has to respond, "I don't know. No reason."

FIG. 12

And the scene can be said to have almost the same effect on the viewer. It is one of the most beautiful, hypnotic, "haunting," and evocative scenes ever filmed, a testimony to the power of erotic presence and to film all at once. (Again, this pairing of a character's reaction and ours courses through all of Hitchcock's work.) The effect is also very much due to the powerful role played by Bernard Herrmann's musical accompaniment to the scene, the first time we hear the "Madeleine or love theme," modeled very closely on the "Liebestod" from Wagner's *Tristan und Isolde*.[63]

The camera moves in on the stained-glass doors of the restaurant, through them, and finds Scottie at the bar leaning back to catch a sight of Madeleine (figure 12). All we hear is the murmur of conversation and other restaurant sounds. Having moved us in and through the doors, the

---

63.   Jack Sullivan points out that however romantic and Wagnerian the music is, especially this "Liebestod" theme, Bernard Herrmann's overall aesthetic is "leaner and more harrowing, is closer to Berlioz." He means the *Symphonie fantastique*, also about "an idealized heroine who brings the hero ecstasy, but also murder, retribution, and self-torment," and whose "actuality is tenuous to begin with." Sullivan, *Hitchcock's Music* (New Haven, CT: Yale University Press, 2006), 222–23. Herrmann's music has become so admired that there is a recording of it (by Varèse Sarabande) giving it the full classical music treatment, and a book-length study that is a bar-by-bar harmonic analysis of every scene in the movie: David Copper, *Bernard Herrmann's "Vertigo": A Film Score Handbook* (Westport: Greenwood, 2001).

camera now pulls our viewing perspective back to a very wide view of the dining room, and begins a left-to-right pan. The furnishings are lush, the most prominent feature being the rich, deep-red brocade wallpaper. (As noted, red and green feature quite prominently in the film, so I will return to that issue.) At the far left, standing out in what is mostly a sea of black, with an occasional muted evening gown worn by the other women, are Elster and the woman Scottie believes is his wife, Madeleine, in a black, backless evening dress, around which a spectacular bright-green wrap is worn (plate 7). We get the sense that Scottie sees her (and is struck by the sight) at the same moment we do. In some way, we are just as struck by her, although we are aided by the slow, dramatic zoom in, accompanied by the lush romantic theme. Perhaps these are cinematic embodiments of how much Scottie is "drawn in" by Madeleine at first sight. We thus see a formal structure that will recur several times. Elster has obviously gone to great lengths to stage this scene, and no doubt he has given some thought to where they will sit, what Scottie will see when he looks at her, and he has instructed her how to exit and where to stop. That is, he has done many of the same things that Hitchcock has done in blocking the scene, such that the viewer and Scottie are paired, observers of a staged scene, but not merely observers; Scottie is pulled in, entranced, by the beauty and allure of the carefully dressed and coiffed Madeleine, as we are by Kim Novak. (And what we see is not a dynamic limited to a murderer plotting the death of his wife and setting up his old friend. Being able to differentiate when what we are seeing, what is being said, is staged for some purpose, is not what it seems to be, is a potential worry that shadows many attempts at mutual understanding. That is part of the reason why it can be a struggle. We don't of course usually encounter anything this extreme, but everyday life is full of persons' attempts to "put one's best foot forward," and that already is a kind of staging.)

As the camera zooms in, there is a cut back to Scottie leaning back to see, and we now see her for the first time from his point of view, as she gets up and gets ready to leave. As she starts moving toward the bar, Scottie must turn to his left to avoid being seen looking at her, but when she stops to wait for Elster and "poses" in a dramatic profile (plate 8), we are not sure if Scottie will continue to turn to his left, or glance back right, especially when she starts to turn to her right, and we sense for a second or two that their eyes might meet. But they don't. Scottie can be completely "taken" with her, without "looking into each other's eyes," something we sense could have happened but did not, another missed connection, and Elster and Madeleine leave for the opera. (We thus have an instance of someone wanting to look without being looked at, turning away rather than being looked at looking. This already seems connected with Scottie's not being able to respond to "Grab my hand" in the opening, and to various hesitations and hedges around Midge.) She more "glides" away than walks, and the camera cuts back to a now pensive Scottie.

This profile shot is meant by Hitchcock to anticipate another, later one, in the midst of Scottie's attempt to convince Judy Barton to allow him to transform her back into Madeleine. When the shot reappears, it is reversed and is shot as a silhouette (plate 9), and again in this later scene, there is a zoom in to the sounds of the Madeleine theme. The reappearance not only suggests a link between Scottie and Elster, as well as with Hitchcock, all three "directors"; it manages to make clear cinematically that Scottie thinks of Judy as a "blank" canvas on which he can project his fantasy, one of many signs of the bullying and manipulative character of the remaking.[64]

This is all it takes for Scottie to be "persuaded," and as we come to learn more about how this one experience so altered Scottie, we are called on to consider the relationship between romantic love and neurotic obsession, or perhaps the suggestion that there is little difference between them. Hitchcock invokes both cinematically and narratively the full mythology of modern romantic love, especially the mysterious power each partner can exert over the other, a power that can be felt instantaneously in a first encounter. To show us this, as noted before, he is invoking elements of the film noir genre both to make this point and, in effect, to quote the cinematic convention, by now well established. He not only makes use of what he knows the audience will believe, but in the elegance and cinematic elaborateness of the staging of the scene, he is also showing us what we will believe, or showing us the mythological status we attribute to "the

64. When the scene is echoed later by the silhouette, it is of course crucial that the "blank" view of Judy (there is no psychological tonality or complexity possible with a silhouette) is from Scottie's point of view.

first time I saw him/her."[65] Again, the convention here is the first sight of the femme fatale in noirs, a scene in which we can see that any semblance of self-direction and control of a future course of action, usually on the part of the man, has been compromised in some way by the power of the encounter. I mean the first appearance of Lana Turner in *The Postman Always Rings Twice* (1946), or Barbara Stanwyck in *Double Indemnity* (1944), or Ava Gardner in *The Killers* (1946), or Rita Hayworth in *The Lady from Shanghai* (1947), or Jane Greer (especially Jane Greer) in *Out of the Past* (1947), or Kathleen Turner in *Body Heat* (1981).

Hitchcock then makes clear his commitment to what he often called "pure cinema," showing as much as possible, rather than saying, by filming fourteen minutes without a word of dialogue. The film cuts directly from the conclusion of the scene at Ernie's to a shot of Scottie waiting in his car outside Madeleine's apartment. Not having any dialogue about his decision to accept Elster's offer reinforces the immediacy and depth of what has happened to Scottie. He has indeed, because of one look, gone from skeptic and rather directionless retired cop to following Madeleine around, as she visits places meant to reinforce the notion that she "has someone inside her" who "wants her to die," as she explains later. She visits a flower shop (Podesta Balocchi, a well-known shop in San Francisco). For the second time in the film, Herrmann's Madeleine theme sounds briefly as Scottie watches her buy the flowers, and our sense from it that he is deeply "hooked" at this point, initially, and more so in subsequent viewings, increases. She purchases there a bouquet identical to that held by Carlotta Valdez in the painting of her hanging in the Legion of Honor museum in the Palace of Fine Arts. In that museum scene, we hear the "Carlotta theme" for the first time, which Herrmann will vary later. (Compare the brilliant, even darker variation on the theme in the redwoods scene, or the equally brilliant use of it in the brief second visit Scottie pays to the museum after his recovery.) She visits a graveyard to contemplate the

---

65. There is this kind of emphasis on the "moment" (and it is discussed as such) in *Spellbound*, in the way the first meeting between the posing Dr. Edwardes (Gregory Peck) and Dr. Peterson (Ingrid Bergman) works its magic. In an early walk together, Dr. Peterson notes the danger of believing the romantic mythology dreamed up by poets, even as it is already clear she has been "stricken" in just the way she disparages.

grave of Carlotta. She visits the museum and sits in front of the portrait. And she disappears into the McKittrick Hotel, which had been the home where Carlotta lived as her paramour's mistress. This last visit Hitchcock leaves deliberately mysterious. Scottie watches Madeleine go in, and sees her clearly at the window, but the landlady claims she hasn't been there that day, and shows Scottie that the key to her room has not been picked up. Scottie visits the room, but there's no Madeleine, and when he looks out the window, there's no Madeleine's car either. There are ways Hitchcock could have made clear how this could have happened. The landlady could have been hired to help, for example. The whacky plot is so full of huge risks, having another confederate involved would be the least of its problems. But, intriguingly, Hitchcock deliberately leaves the event inexplicable, perhaps suggesting that there is some link or parallelism between what we are willing to accept of the illusions created in cinema and Scottie's increasing willingness to believe there might be something not rationally explicable in what is happening to Madeleine. People speak casually of the "magic" of cinema all the time, but what Hitchcock leaves us with looks only explicable by, literally, some sort of magic.[66]

6. POP LEIBEL

Scottie next breezes back into Midge's apartment. He has discovered a name associated now with all four of the places to which he has followed Madeleine—Carlotta Valdez—and, detective that he is, he wants to investigate. He asks Midge for the name of someone who knows the fine-grained social history of San Francisco, and she and he head off to the Argosy Bookshop, run by one Pop Leibel. He tells them the story of Carlotta Valdez, emphasizing that, however sad, it is not an "unusual story," and again, that "there are many such stories," this story of a rich man bringing a very young girl up from somewhere south of the city (the San Juan Bau-

---

66. Of course, it is also the case that Hitchcock, for all the care he lavished on his films, was generally indifferent to ensuring absolute consistency in the plots, even after someone pointed out a problem.

tista mission that will play a large role later) to be his mistress. They had a child, and the man grew tired of Carlotta, took the child, and "threw her away." "A man could do that in those days. They had the power and the freedom," Pop says, invoking the phrase we have heard Elster use, and will hear again one more time. In fact, thanks to Elster's power and money, this is just what he does with Judy Barton when finished with the murder plot: the "usual"—he "threw her away." With her child stolen from her, Carlotta went mad, and finally took her own life.

Once again, we should note an emphasis on a general characteristic of a specific social world—the presence of a kind of power (money) and the freedom, and the independence it buys, to act as one wants to, and a corresponding dependence by others with little or no money. Both descriptions early in the film purport to describe a past social world, but that is an ironic qualification. Elster's successful machinations show that the same kind of hierarchy still exists, only in a more disguised, less openly brutal, but now quite manipulative way. In such a world, now requiring such deceit, but with the same relations of dependence, discerning the difference between staged or manipulating and authentic is ever more complicated. Those without such power and freedom must take great care about how they are perceived, and must often disguise their true reactions to the powerful. Mutual interpretability becomes a task, a struggle, and given the motivations for succeeding by accommodating to such a world, the odds that expressions of self-knowledge are expressions of self-deceit are quite high.[67]

On the ride home, Midge is eager to hear the whole story, having deduced from what little Scottie has told her that it was Elster who engaged him and that Elster believes Carlotta has come back from the dead to haunt his wife. It is another indication that despite Scottie's unwillingness to joke about the ludicrousness of this premise, and despite his reserve in

67.   I admit that suggesting this interpretive framework (the problems that arise in situations of manifold dependencies among beings who highly value their independence) as a way of understanding the uncertainties that arise because of theatricalized public personae would require considerable expansion before its historical dimensions and fine-grained structure could be made clearer. But for our purposes, I mean to refer to such obvious contexts as, to choose just one example, our insistence, for reasons that are deeply important to us, that our political institutions be democratic, but the corporate world is hierarchical and often authoritarian. Tension, at the very least, is to be expected.

the conversation, Midge does not see that Scottie is taking all this quite seriously, is not responding to her "Oh, come on, Johnny." She has known Scottie a long time, so we have to assume that this is all very untypical of him. He seems to have lost the contempt he originally expressed about the premise, but Midge, in a way again typical of her, does not see that, even though we can clearly see Scottie's discomfort with her tone, and we can see his reserve, all of which she could see as well, but does not. She merrily says she is going to go see this portrait, and the camera lingers for a while with Scottie in the car, pensive and quite serious. He picks up the museum catalogue again and flips to the picture of Carlotta, and Hitchcock superimposes the Ernie's profile shot of Madeleine, suggesting what thought Scottie is at least entertaining, that Carlotta and Madeleine are one person, or that one can transform into the other.

Scottie reports to Elster at a gentleman's club, and Elster tells him the whole story, that Carlotta Valdez was Madeleine's great-grandmother, that the child, her grandmother, also committed suicide in 1857, that Madeleine now takes out some of Carlotta's jewelry that she inherited and looks at it, and he shocks Scottie by claiming that Madeleine knows nothing of all this history, is visiting these places without knowing what she is doing and without remembering. When Scottie expresses astonishment and asks how she knows to do all this, Elster replies that when she leaves home on these wanderings, "she is no longer my wife." This is of course as rich and typical an example of Hitchcockian irony as Norman Bates's famous "Mother is not herself today" line from *Psycho*. That is, Elster is lying by telling the truth. Judy Barton is certainly not his wife when she leaves home for the Carlotta places. Since Scottie and the fake Madeleine will soon begin what Scottie must believe to be an adulterous affair, one that Elster has planned to happen, it is also significant for the plan that he says "she is not my wife." It is not quite permission to have the affair, but is likely not unrelated to what he is subtly encouraging Scottie to do.

The resonance of this line with the one in *Psycho* (or, rather, *Psycho*'s resonance with it, since *Psycho* was two years later) suggests a deeper connection between the two films, since both feature a character haunted by, burdened by, the past, as if a character from the past can "inhabit" or take over a present character. Of course, in this case, that haunting is phony, staged, but it appears again with some irony when Judy tries desperately not to be, to escape and leave behind, the burden of "the Judy who pretended to be Madeleine and seduced Scottie." And that general theme appears frequently in other Hitchcock films too, suggesting he sees a common problem in human life: how to bear properly, appropriately, either the burden of the past, of what one inherits and cannot escape, or the burden of one's own past, what one has done. It is the central element in *Notorious*, as Cary Grant's censorious and moralistic character cannot bring himself to believe that Ingrid Bergman's character can ever become anything other than the promiscuous party girl he knew her as (a "tramp" is his word for her), and she cannot easily believe that he could ever finally trust her to have changed.[68] It is an issue in *North by Northwest*, again as an issue of forgiveness and reconciliation. Somehow Cary Grant's character in that film finds a way to trust Eva Marie Saint's character, even though she once collaborated in a plot to murder him, and was the mistress of an evil spy before she was turned by the government to work against him.[69] And it is *the* central issue in *Marnie*, with its suggestion (and it is just a suggested possibility, and a fairly faint one) that coming to *understand* the past is one way, not of breaking with it and leaving it behind, but of bearing it in a new and more successful way.

7. IN THE BAY AND IN SCOTTIE'S APARTMENT

The next two scenes are among the most important in the film. The next day, Scottie follows Madeleine again, and this time he watches her drive near the San Francisco Bay, with the Golden Gate Bridge as a backdrop.

68. This is just plot summary. What Devlin knows, and knows that he knows, and what he knows, but manages to avoid knowing that he knows, are among the most interesting psychological dimensions of the film.

69. In *Notorious*, Cary Grant's character, Devlin, does not so much as really forgive Alicia, Ingrid Bergman's character, as own up to his own coresponsibility for what she was doing, sleeping with Alexander. There is a marvelously ambiguous smile on Bergman's face in the last scene of the film, after her rescue and their reconciliation. It is motherly, rather than romantic, as if she is gratified that this immature moralist has finally become an adult, and as if she is amused that it has taken him "rescuing" her to make this happen.

(This is already a kind of cinematic qualification on the upcoming fake suicide attempt, something Scottie could have seen had he been capable of playing his detective role, rather than the "smitten victim of the plot" character. The Golden Gate Bridge was, at the time of the film, the most heavily used suicide bridge in the States. Had Madeleine really been interested in suicide, we can clearly see what decisive option was open to her.)[70] He sees her stroll distractedly by the bay, at Fort Point, by the southern entrance to the Golden Gate Bridge, and watches her as she tears petals off the bouquet of flowers she had bought the day before (something that will return as an image in a later dream/nightmare he has). But then he watches in horror as she nonchalantly jumps into the bay in an apparent suicide attempt. He dives in after her and carries her to his car. All the while, of course, she is pretending to have attempted suicide and pretends to be in and out of consciousness. What is no pretense, however, is the intensity of Scottie's anxiety and passion as he tries to revive her in the car, going well beyond any Good Samaritan concern. We see other mythological or even fantasy conventions invoked, especially the *rescuing male/saving a woman* (or Cinderella or Sleeping Beauty) fantasy, which plays such a large role in *Notorious* and *Marnie* and is a major counterpoint to his relationship with Midge, who perhaps seems unattractive to him because she does not need "saving," is a stable, mature, rational woman. It is another dimension of the delicate dynamic between independence and dependence we have started to explore, especially its role in romantic relationships, where it can quickly become, let us say, unbalanced. For our purposes, we just need to note that the moment of Scottie's first expression of far more than mere concern (plate 10) occurs after this staged suicide and his rescue. Elster and Judy Barton know what they are doing.

Remarkably, Scottie does not seek medical attention for Madeleine, but takes her back to his apartment. (Perhaps he already has something in mind.) Madeleine continues throughout to pretend that she is

---

70. This is an issue for Mark (Sean Connery) in *Marnie* when Marnie (Tippi Hedren) attempts suicide in the ship pool, even though they are sailing on an ocean. Mark remarks on this fact, and she has a snappy comeback, that the idea was to kill herself, not feed the fishes. Such bantering would be out of place in *Vertigo*, which, aside from the brief scenes with Midge, is as uniformly serious a film as *I Confess* or *The Wrong Man*.

FIG. 13

unconscious, and so allows Scottie, probably worried about hypothermia, to completely undress her and put her to bed. We know this because after they reach his place we see the inside of Scottie's apartment: small, tidy when compared to Midge's, modest when compared to Elster's office or Madeleine's Jaguar or the gentleman's club. Scottie's has the air of a man who has lived alone all his life. A right-to-left pan shows her clothes, all of them, undergarments included, hanging on a line in the kitchen and then shows us her sleeping, naked, in what is obviously his bed (figure 13). If Scottie had not been a big boy before, big enough to know what brassieres are, he certainly is now.

A phone call awakens Madeleine (or she decides that she has pretended long enough), and there is an awkward scene as she goes through the motions of pretending to realize that she is naked and in a strange man's bed (figure 14).

He leaves her alone, after giving her his robe to put on, and in a few seconds she makes an entrance carefully choreographed by Hitchcock to foreshadow the most emotionally charged entrance in the film, when Judy reappears from the bathroom as, once again fully, Scottie's beloved Madeleine. The Madeleine musical theme is even used for the apartment entrance, even though the major theme, in true Wagnerian fashion, is not fully resolved here (it is "suspended"), but only, finally, in the later "apparition"

FIG. 14

of Madeleine, one has to call it. Again we see the red-green contrast, the Madeleine who initially aroused this great, powerful passion in red, and the mysterious, remade, magical Madeleine bathed in green light (plates 11 and 12). These are, with respect to our theme, beautifully thought-out "framing" scenes. It is when she is naked that Judy is at her most deceptive, and it is when elaborately remade and clothed by Scottie that the genuineness of Judy's love for Scottie can be seen and reciprocated.[71]

This and what follows are one of many instances where everything changes upon multiple viewings. On the first viewing, we are drawn into the unusual and, we think, accidental intimacy between them and what seems to be a budding love affair, all by conventional movie cues, especially the musical score and the intimate setting. (This is not to deny that there is also something clearly already overwrought and unsettling about Scottie's behavior.) But on a second viewing, as we realize that what Madeleine is doing is staged and manipulative, we also realize that Scottie does not reveal to her who he is or why he is following her, and also acts in a way

71.   This introduces the idea of a dialectical relation between "inner" and "outer" that is perfectly Hegelian: "Hence what is only something inner, is also thereby only external, and what is only external is also only something inner." G. W. F. Hegel, *The Encyclopedia Logic*, trans. T. F. Geraets, W. A. Suchting, and H. S. Harris (Indianapolis: Hackett, 1991), 197.

that clearly goes well beyond what his task requires. We note his striking lack of response to her mentioning "I'm married, you know." We note that the active-passive relation, which seemed uncomfortably completely one-sided (we are asked to imagine Scottie undressing a limp, unconscious Madeleine, a grotesque version of a male fantasy about a fully compliant, unresisting woman), now seems completely one-sided in the *other* direction, as Scottie is the one manipulated. Perhaps on a third viewing, however, we suspect that for both parties, something is beginning between them, on her side as well, that cannot be wholly explained by her role, or Scottie's part, in the plot.[72]

It is the deception going on here, by Elster, Judy, and even Scottie, that creates the near comical number of self- and other-representations sketched previously. Each persona, how one is trying to be perceived, is a publicly presented self-representation[73] that can range from conscious and sincere, to conscious and insincere, to conscious, sincere, but unsuccessful (no one takes you to be who you give them to think you are), all the way to unconscious and unsuccessful (you have a false idea of how you are perceived, and no access to why you are presenting yourself a certain way, and "have no clue," we sometimes say, about how what you do *is* perceived). And there are similar variations on how and why one is represented in some way *by others*, some others, or a particular other, many of them not motivated by wanting to see rightly but by some other desire or

72. It is certainly true that Judy/Madeleine knows how to flirt. When Scottie asks her if this has ever happened to her before, she hesitates until he explains: "fall into San Francisco Bay." She gives a short "Oh . . ." and pauses slightly, before she says no, clearly indicating that she took him to mean "Have you ever awakened naked in a strange man's bed?" By giving this little hint, she is also alluding to that possibility, or rather the actuality she finds herself in, and is treating it in a lighthearted way, hinting that it is an acceptable thought, not one she recoils from in moral indignation.

73. The artifice is emphasized in the film by attention to clothes, hair color, and hair style, by Judy's accent (and Kim Novak's extraordinary ability to switch subtly between Madeleine's upper-crust and Judy's Kansas accent), and by the fact that Judy is, of course, a makeup artist at Magnin. She will not let Scottie kiss her because she just "put her face on." Submitting to what she must be, must look like, dress like, in order for Scottie to love her is clearly also a general figure for what women are obliged to do for men: play out the role of their fantasy. (I don't know quite what to make of the fact, but clearly some connection is intended between Midge's job designing ad copy for lingerie, in particular a cantilevered bra, and the fact that we first see Madeleine's bare back and that Judy is bra-less in all the scenes we see of her.)

need or interest. All these possibilities establish the vertiginous unknow-ingness of Hitchcock's world.

We know that Scottie is misrepresenting himself to Madeleine as a wanderer who just happened to come across her, and not a detective hired by her husband, and we sense that he will quickly begin a deception of Elster, who he has no reason to think is anything but an old college buddy full of concern for his increasingly insane wife. The deception is imminent since it is already likely that he will soon begin what he, at least, will believe is an adulterous affair with that wife. In some sense or other, he already has begun by the signal he gives her in not responding at all to her declaration that she is married. In fact, as far as we can tell from everything we see, Scottie completely forgets about Elster hereafter, does not mention him again, and apart from one last phone call (as Madeleine hurriedly dresses and leaves) reports no more to him. Elster vanishes from the movie until the murder and the coroner's inquest. The moment of intimacy, which, on first viewing, we are tempted to think is a genuine spark between them, occurs at the end of their conversation, when the phone rings again, and their hands touch and linger (plate 13).

This apartment scene is clearly meant to contrast with the scene in Midge's apartment. Those strains of tension and miscommunication seem here replaced by an instant ease with each other and some rapidly growing intimacy, even though "seems" is the operative word. A noted, they are both deceiving each other, and Scottie is about to begin his deceit of Elster. To add once again to the complexity, this sort of deception is vaguely but unmistakably echoed in *what Hitchcock does to us the viewer*, inviting us to believe the surface narrative, to experience genuine shock and sadness at Madeleine's suicide, and to feel sympathy for Scottie's profound, debil-itating sadness at Madeleine's death, to sympathize with and worry about his convalescence, even as Hitchcock knows that he himself will, fairly late in the movie, reveal to us that everything we have seen was staged by him and was illusory, as staged as what Elster and Judy are doing to Scottie.[74]

---

74. About "what Madeleine is" in the film, Gregg Horowitz says that she is "not a woman, but Scot-tie's own unmastered past, massively displaced onto and disguised as the image of a woman who is herself a fiction constructed by another man" ("Made-to-Order Witness," 125). What Horowitz says about the status of Madeleine for Scottie is largely true, but not, it seems to me, completely true. It

In a film so filled with doublings and repetitions, this one, the doubling of Scottie and his passage through unknowingness and the audience's similar journey (which evokes the Hitchcock-Elster doubling) may be the most important, and may have the most general significance, figuring what Katie Trumpener describes as "the film's twisting of levels, and its ultimate self-consuming collapse," which "suggest simultaneously the fragility of such constructions [she means the notion, quite rightly, *very* broadly: 'institutions,' 'social systems,' 'cinematic apparatuses']; the moment of self-replication is the moment at which the system at once demonstrates its power most confidently, and exposes itself to the greatest risks."[75]

But in general, despite these complications, we viewers have no trouble thinking in these terms although we also assume that they have a commonsensical limit. On the first viewing of the film, we want to accept the romantic mythology that Scottie has somehow connected and begun to fall in love with the real person, the person who he eventually learns was Judy Barton all along, and not so much a person under some description. In many such cases, we like to say that there is clearly some "chemistry" between them because we want to be able to say that the "spark" between them is independent of the various descriptions available as we get to know someone.[76] We want to insist: one loves "the person him- or herself,"

---

is true to the extent that such a projection of one's past is true of any romantic relationship. But this is only possible with a certain person, not anyone, and such a person reacts, engages, resists, and so forth. The relationship is dynamic and fluid, and can admit of several levels of self-consciousness.

75.   Katie Trumpener, "Fragments of the Mirror: Self-Reference, *Mise en Abyme, Vertigo*," in *Hitchcock's Rereleased Films: From "Rope" to "Vertigo*," ed. Walter Raubichek and Walter Srebnick (Detroit, MI: Wayne State University Press, 1993), 187. Another phrase for such a self-undermining dynamic is Hegel's notion of dialectical negation, an internal or determinate negation that is most visible in the account of sociality evoked by Rousseau earlier here. As with the case of Makkai's use of Sartre later (see note 105), it seems to me more perspicuous to bring out the philosophical dimensions of this phenomenon not by reference to what Trumpener calls "the Althusserian model of subject formation," but by reference to his origin, Hegel's account.

76.   It would seem strangely restrictive to say that Scottie can love "the haunted wife of Elster," but would not be able to fall in love with "Judy who is pretending to be haunted," that he does not love the woman under that description. That *is* "whom" he falls in love with! This would be one plausible explanation for the fact that even after he knows the plot and is dealing with "Judy the fake Madeleine," his love seems to reemerge. (In the last moments of the film, knowing everything, he nevertheless says to Judy, "I loved you so, Madeleine.") For he is dealing throughout with "the woman" whom he fell in love with and knew as Madeleine. The issue is not straightforward though. A wife

bearer of multiple possible descriptions. They both, we think or hope, can somehow feel their way through any artificial personae created by the plot and by Scottie's deception of Madeleine, and fall in love, the most important fall in a movie full of them.[77] But after Scottie thinks that Madeleine is dead, and finds and begins to "rebuild" Judy back into Madeleine, the *object* of his love, the object of his care and desire, seems to have much more to do with voice, clothes, hair style, and hair color than any "real person." Although much has been made of the possibility that Scottie's love for the dead Madeleine borders on necrophilia,[78] this can miss the irony of Scottie's refashioning project (not to mention that what Scottie wants to do is to make love to a reborn or alive Madeleine, not a dead one). But that project suggests that any such "real" persona as we have been discussing can be in reality something as mysterious and disturbing as a mere "look," or dress, or hairstyle (or scent, or profile, or gait, or, indeed someone's back, at some moment, in some context), an instigation of a projected fantasy, not a revelation of "the person" to be loved.[79] In this context, Judy's later

---

may love her "faithful husband," but the love may disappear when she faces the "betraying husband." Or not; the love may well, often does, survive. And a woman who loves her husband qua faithful may avow that she would not love her husband qua betrayer, but then find that the situation is much more complicated, and that she still does love him.

77.   This is related to, although not exactly the same as, a familiar variant: a lover who learns something about the beloved's past, but comes to believe that such actions are not reflections of the real person, the person he or she loves. A woman falling for an ex-gunfighter and a man falling for an ex-prostitute are movie staples, as are many "Mary Magdalene" conversion cases. Cf. also Trumpener's apposite formulation: "in *Vertigo*, falling in love turning into loved ones falling—every hierarchy collapsing." Trumpener, "Fragments of the Mirror," 180.

78.   This is something suggested by Hitchcock. See François Truffaut, *Le cinéma selon Hitchcock* (Paris: Robert Laffont, 1966). It is certainly true, though, that Hitchcock's films are suffused with death, anxiety about death, and different sorts of attempts to deny death. Cf. *Rope* (1948), *Psycho*, *The Trouble with Harry*.

79.   As already noted, in a movie with a main character named Madeleine, with names like Elster (cf. the painter, Elstir, in the novel), and which is about a search for lost time, this is a Proustian theme. Cf. "When we are in love with a woman we simply project on to her a state of our own soul. It is only a clumsy and erroneous form of perception which places everything in the object, when really everything is in the mind." Marcel Proust, *Remembrance of Things Past*, trans. C. K. Scott Moncrieff and Terence Kilmartin (London: Chatto and Windus, 1981), 1:891/833 and 3:950/912. Proust's novel takes the mystery of romantic love to an extreme with the Swann and Odette story, making credible the claim that one can love someone whom one does not even like, who is, as Swann memorably says, not even his "type."

plea to be loved "as she really is" can sound naïve. But this is so only up to a point. Anxiety about being loved "for who one really is" is hardly an uncommon anxiety. And the important role suggested for fantasy in romantic love can imply (and in this film certainly does imply) that one is always enthralled to a fictional or absent (or "dead") person, the fantastical person whom one takes the other to be, the object of the apparently necessary fantasy; in a word, "Madeleine."[80]

The psychological dynamics involved in these personae and especially their shifting self-representations, shifting as the other's shifts, is at the heart of the film's greatness. But there is another odd feature of the film throughout that should be noted here and returned to later. A premise for this feature is a well-known aspect of the image (or myth) of romantic love—that it is "beautiful," has a kind of moral beauty. What is usually meant is that there is a kind of desire and regard for another that completely transcends self-interest and all aspects of egoism, and so involves a mutual dedication to the other's happiness and well-being, even if at the expense of one's own. (So in some accounts, the love is even purer, more an expression of what love truly is, if it is unrequited, accepted as such, but the love maintains its intensity. One still loves, "from afar.") Such a love may be instigated by a great passion and a desire for physical intimacy with another, but if that desire is not an expression of such a regard and respect for the other, if it is not reciprocated in the same register by the other, then the result is what the self-help books call "mutual pleasuring," with none of the ideal beauty of romantic love. Since such love also exposes one to rejection and manipulation if it is not reciprocated, it also requires a level of trust as great as, if not greater than, any such relation in human life. And since what all of this demands sets such a high bar, this link with the beautiful introduces, virtually demands, the role of fantasy in romantic relationships, the idealizations and sheer extraordinariness, the almost willful creation of mystery and distance, insisted on by love poems,

---

80.   Absences in Hitchcock's work could be the theme of another book, whether as McGuffins (objects devoutly desired but often not named, the significance of which is not explained, or explained in a way that is not proportional to the intensity of the desire for them), as unknowns or hidden meanings in something seen, or, most often, as the (eternal) absence of any satisfying sense that one is loved.

songs, and romantic rituals.[81] Any putative love, with no aura of mystery, vulnerability, and strangeness created and sustained by the imagination, no imaginative attention to the beauty of the relationship, can be a pedestrian thing.[82] (Hence the contrasting relationship with Midge—perhaps what "love" looks like without the fantasy.)

An implication of this insistence on the moral beauty of romantic love is that a strategy to take advantage of such a romantic expectation for one's own advantage or mere pleasure, pretending a commitment to the romantic narrative for mere gain, is, in the moral sense, an ugly thing, one of the ugliest of human capacities. This is, of course, exactly what Judy is doing by pretending to be Madeleine and seducing, by pretending to fall for, Scottie. Since, for most of the film, we don't, on first viewing, know that this is what is happening, no serious moral issue arises, and when we do learn the truth, events unfold so rapidly that it is all we can do simply to catch up. But after we do learn the truth, any moral revulsion seems somehow reduced by our belief that she finally did "fall for him" as the romantic narrative requires. We learn the truth only when it can also be established that Judy has sustained her love for Scottie. (And we are never shown any scene between Judy and Elster together, plotting, something that would surely stir some revulsion.) By contrast, the Madeleine fiction created by Elster and Judy to ensnare Scottie is a paradigm of such ugliness, the Carlotta Valdez story. Pop Leibel and Scottie and Midge are clearly affected by the injustice and cruelty of such a story, as no doubt are we.

81.   The fantasy theme is also interlocked throughout with the theme of art. The connections between love, art, beauty, and fantasy make up a constant undercurrent throughout the plot development, and are obviously especially relevant to cinema's erotic power and its beautiful stars. This theme is given an insightful treatment by Nickolas Pappas in "Magic and Art in *Vertigo*," chap. 2 in Makkai, *Vertigo*.

82.   Cf. the telling remarks of Stanley Cavell: "It is a poor idea of fantasy which takes it to be a world apart from reality, a world clearly showing its unreality. Fantasy is precisely what reality can be confused with. It is through fantasy that our conviction of the worth of reality is established; to forgo our fantasies would be to forgo our touch with the world. And does someone claim to know the specific balance sanity must sustain between the elaborating demands of self and world, some neat way of keeping soul and body together?" Cavell, *The World Viewed*, 85. And as Victor Perkins puts it, "Fantasy is at the same time dangerous and essential. In Hitchcock's world, a man's moral and psychological integrity, even his physical existence, is threatened by precisely those desires and illusions which make life tolerable." Perkins, *Film as Film: Understanding and Judging Movies* (New York: Penguin Books, 1972), 154.

The romantic element is a familiar plot device in Hollywood movies, as well as Shakespeare: what starts out as a ruse or a strategy or a joke develops into real love, but then cannot be believed, must face some crisis or test to be believed.[83] But something about the intensity of the romantic developments and the state of unknowingness of the characters seems to push aside somehow any moment of what, for us and for the characters, we would understand as the relevance of moral categories.[84] This suspension, or perhaps our willingness to suspend, is highlighted by the fact that the one character in the film full of moral certainty and righteousness, the

83. Not to mention another Hollywood frame that this one fits: an older man trying to re-create with a younger woman a fading memory of a passion that has, in this case literally, gone dead. This mythic frame fits any lover futilely trying to find some way to re-create, to experience again, the first moments of a love affair, as doomed an attempt as trying to watch *Vertigo*, the film one saw on first viewing, again. Any second or third viewing is of another film; any reanimation of a love affair is just that, some staged reanimation, not "the" first experience. The language of "too late" and "second chances" is interwoven through the film and is especially prominent in the closing scenes. The repetition of the past, especially when suffused with obsession, is of course a Freudian "frame" as well. (It is often said that there can be no comparable "second viewing" of the film, once we know the truth. But there is really no true "first viewing" either. It would be more correct to say that our first time through just lays the groundwork for the genuine experience of the film: the second [and future] viewing, the true first viewing. All of this in the same sense that all great literature is read in order to be reread.)

84. In itself this peculiarity is not all that unusual in Hitchcock's films. In *Marnie*, a movie "literally" about a thief, the context created makes the application of that term simplistic. As in many of his movies, the qualification, the context that makes that and other moral terms superficial, is psychological. In *Shadow of a Doubt*, at the end of the film, the young girl Charlie knows (because of a discovery of a telltale ring) that her uncle Charlie is indeed the Merry Widow murderer, and as Hitchcock films her descending a staircase, he highlights the ring (what she knows), then shows us that Uncle Charles knows that she knows, and also that Uncle Charles has set up his next victim for murder. But Charlie keeps quiet, because she knows how important her uncle is to his sister, her mother. There is no ambiguity about this; she knows the murder may well occur if she does nothing, and although she is unquestionably a "good person" throughout, she is willing to let this happen, and it has to be said that Hitchcock treats this sympathetically. This is noted in the chapter on *Shadow of a Doubt* in William Rothman's *Hitchcock: The Murderous Gaze* (Cambridge: Cambridge University Press, 1984), 243. See also the discussion of this scene by George Wilson, "Interpretation," in *The Routledge Companion to Film and Philosophy*, ed. Paisley Livingston and Carl Plantinga (Oxford: Routledge, 2009), 168–70. It is certainly safe to say that Hitchcock's world is not a morally organized world. The evil prosper, the innocent suffer, and the slightly culpable, like Scottie, are visited with misery all out of proportion. See Durgnat, *The Strange Case of Alfred Hitchcock*, 284.

coroner (or judge; it is not clear) at the inquest, is a smug, self-satisfied prig who has understood nothing about either the facts or anyone's motivations. It is not infrequent in Hitchcock's films that the voice of morality is such a posing, strutting fraud.[85]

8. TWO ARE GOING SOMEWHERE

As Madeleine leaves the apartment, whom should we see pull up but Midge, in her cute sports car.[86] (An interesting bit of flair that suggests Hitchcock is showing us that we are probably underestimating Midge, have not read her well.) Her arrival can hardly be accidental, but we do not know if she visits Scottie as casually and unannounced as he visits her, or if she was checking up on him. Her tone as she speaks to herself suggests the latter. A sarcastic look and tone are evident as she asks out loud, "Well, Johnny-O, was it a ghost? Was it fun?" (figure 15). It is also not clear whether in this case she actually understands Scottie better than he understands himself, or whether she thinks he has been dishonest with her. That is, does she realize that Scottie's explanation of what he is doing (he had said to her the night before in response to her incredulity, "I'm not telling you what I believe; I'm telling you what *he* believes"), helping a friend, is self-deceived and that he is committed to some aspect of the Carlotta story, or smitten with Madeleine, or both? Or does she think he has not so much been dishonest with himself, but simply with her? Her wounded and somewhat bitter tone suggests the latter, but in either case, she is wounded. This (another source of misunderstanding) is important to remember because she will only have two more scenes in the drama: back in her apartment, when she shows her "Johnny" the painting with her head on Carlotta's body, and

---

85.   Another good example of this: Cary Grant's character's smug moral contempt for Ingrid Bergman's character throughout most of *Notorious*. The irony of him trying to persuade her to do exactly what he condemns her for is not lost on her. See also the rather extreme irony in the minister's final remarks about Uncle Charlie in *Shadow of a Doubt*.

86.   It is a 1956 Karmann Ghia, the Volkswagen sports car. Scottie's car is a utilitarian 1956 DeSoto, and Madeleine's is a 1957 Jaguar.

FIG. 15

in Scottie's hospital room after his breakdown. In the former, she is certainly miscalculating Scottie's response and is stunned when he walks out on her, but in this case that may well have occurred because she is angry and the sarcasm implicit in the painting is an attempt to strike back, the effectiveness of which she had seriously underestimated. One has the sense that she has never had a serious rival before.

At any rate, the next morning, Scottie is back at his post, following Madeleine, but is quite puzzled by her route, until he realizes she is driving back to his apartment. (Another spiral returning after a loop, circling around its origin; all roads from Scottie lead—for Scottie—back to Scottie, a feature of his isolated narcissism.) She has come to leave a thank-you note, and the same flirtatious, easy banter resumes, even about her nakedness. (Scottie had tried to say that he enjoyed talking with her, but in context at that moment, the reference in "I enjoyed it" seemed to both of them to be undressing her.)

She prepares to leave and he clearly does not want her to go, and they begin talking about wandering again. He tells her it would be a waste to wander separately, and there ensues dialogue that Scottie can't quite follow. She is trying to tell him something important and suggestive that he can't pick up on. She says, "Only one is a wanderer, two together are always going somewhere." She is a married woman, and he knows this. She is in effect saying, "If you get in this car with me, we are going somewhere, you and I, the same place. And we both know where." Ever slow on the uptake, Scottie responds by saying that is not necessarily so, as if they can go on just "wandering" without being committed to any "destination." The decision is made when she issues another clever double entendre about his vulnerability, what he is leaving himself open to: "You left your door open." He closes it (the door, not what she means) and off they go.[87]

In general, wandering is an important (and persistent) metaphor in itself, from the first time it is introduced, in Midge's apartment, to the end of the film. Wandering is an expression of a desire, a dissatisfaction with staying put, a quest, but for something one cannot specify. One wanders hoping to find what one is looking for, without ex ante knowing what it is. Scottie, in the brilliant portrayal by Stewart, is a virtually complete embodiment of longing, yearning, what the German Romantics might even call "infinite" striving, endlessly dissatisfied but always striving nonetheless. Madeleine tries to tell him: by coming with me you *are* clearly indicating what you want. Scottie, typical of him, still resists acknowledging even that—as if it is not that he doesn't know what he wants, but, again typically, will not admit it to himself.[88]

9. SEMPER VIRENS

There then ensues the strangest, moodiest scene in the film.[89] They drive out to a redwood forest and stroll among the giant sequoias. It is here that

87. "Double entendre? All the gestures, looks, phrases, in *Vertigo* have a double meaning." Marker, "A Free Replay," 125.

88. Cf. Stanley Cavell's comment: "*Vertigo* is just a movie, but no other movie I know so purely conveys the sealing of a mind within a scorching fantasy. James Stewart is not much of an antihero, but the totality of his longing—and the terrorizing defacement of his object's identity which his longing comes to require—mimics that convulsion of consciousness which transcends idolatry in favor of the fantastic reality of God, that point past imagination at which happiness and truth coalesce." Cavell, *The World Viewed*, 86.

89. They are in the Big Basin Redwoods State Park. For a rich account of the role of the scene in the film, see Tom Gunning, "The Desire and the Pursuit of the Hole: Cinema's Obscure Object of Desire," in Bartsch and Bartscherer, *Erotikon*, 261–77. Gunning sees the indifference of the ages to

Madeleine for the first time goes into her full Carlotta act, adopting a far-away, vacant, slightly dazed look, and giving Scottie to believe that Carlotta is present, inhabiting Madeleine. It begins when she says that she "doesn't like it, knowing I have to die," brought to this thought by the number of humans who have lived and died in the two thousand years the trees have been alive. Scottie has told her that their scientific name is *Sequoia semper-virens*, "ever green," "ever living." (It can mean both.)

They stop by an exhibit of the cross section of one of the trees that had been cut down in 1930 with dates marked on the rings to show significant events, as far back as 909. Madeleine points to a small gap and says, "There I was born, there I died. It was only a moment for you. You took no notice." This is the first time she has spoken to Scottie as the dead Carlotta, and she effectively "channels" what she understandably assumes to be Carlotta's bitterness at the great indifference of the cosmos, the whole ancient cyclical order of things, to her miserable fate: "You (that is, no one at all) took no notice." The repetitive, unchanging cycle of time is another meaning of the signature spirals. They could take my child and throw me away, and they can still do that now. No one notices, the cosmos is indifferent to such pain, and it is unending, this cycle of men abusing and throwing away women. The implication seems to be "Best come join me in death. Wherever you are heading, the cycle will continue, the abuse, pain, and indifference will return inevitably." She wanders off in a daze and Scottie follows, tries to get her to discuss where she thinks she is, who she thinks she is. She makes a show of struggling to regain control, is in some emotional pain, and walks toward the ocean, which, given recent history, is a dangerous spot for Carlotta-haunted Madeleine. As they converse and she tells him of her dream, she plants the seed of "the tower," probably in Spain, she says; the first step in getting Scottie to the site of the murder. Scottie thinks

the human struggle for love, and so to the ceaseless attempts and endless failures of love, in terms of the Aristophanic myth in Plato's *Symposium* of human existence as a constant quest for a lost wholeness (the "circle men"): that we believe love will be satisfying if we can find our other half, the unique being in the universe who will "complete" us. I agree that what Gunning notes as the film's "ever increasing reputation" is due to the realization that its concerns are very large, nothing less than "both the pathology and the emotional depth of Love as pursued in the Western tradition" (266). See also the discussion by Robin Wood in his chapter on *Vertigo* in *Hitchcock's Films Revisited*, 114–16.

PLATE 1

PLATE 2

PLATE 3

PLATE 4

PLATE 5

PLATE 6

PLATE 7

PLATE 8

PLATE 9

PLATE 10

PLATE 11

PLATE 12

PLATE 13

PLATE 14

PLATE 15

PLATE 16

PLATE 17

PLATE 18

PLATE 19

PLATE 20

PLATE 21

PLATE 22

PLATE 23

PLATE 24

he can find "the key" to all these symbols in her dream, broken mirrors, open graves, walking into darkness. She runs closer to the rocky shoreline, he follows, they embrace, and she says there is someone within her who says she must die and she doesn't want to. This scene is their first kiss and the beginning of their affair, and for any viewer, on the first viewing of the film, it is a scene loaded, clearly deliberately overloaded, with romantic symbolism: they kiss just as a huge wave hits the rocks in climactic fashion (plate 14). It is as if Hitchcock is not only deceiving the audience and manipulating their emotions, but also having some fun with these romantic conventions, coming close to explicitly mocking what the gullible audience is willing to accept, even the crashing waves in the background. (He appears to be having as much fun with these romantic conventions as when he has fireworks going off behind Cary Grant and Grace Kelly in *To Catch a Thief* [1955].) It is hard to realize as we watch such a symbolically charged scene that, again, *everything* we see from Madeleine is false. She is calculatingly seducing Scottie in perfect conformity with the plot, acting out a vulnerability that is a lie, even as she is apparently, as we learn later, actually falling in love with him.

On the other hand, she has introduced the romantic theme of the relation between love and death, appropriate for a movie whose score evokes so constantly the "Liebestod" in *Tristan und Isolde*. That is, this evocation of an imminent mortality greatly intensifies the stakes in Scottie's relation to Madeleine. On some accounts, accounts in which two become one, love is itself a kind of death, a self-forgetfulness and transcendence of all ego in a merging with another. In others, this moment of early love so perfectly embodies the reality of love, and so soon will be worn down by habit and the quotidian, that the perfect love is the love of young lovers who die at the moment of their greatest, most intense experience of their love, before the love itself has a chance to die. Here the idea that Madeleine's life is in danger makes a decision by Scottie to "be there always" for her obvious and unavoidable, despite any risks. The scene is overdone to emphasize the fantasy aspect (and that in itself is a kind of warning to viewers about their own credulity in watching film), but the romantic scene is not completely parodied, and this emotional "acceleration" of their love is compelling on its own, despite the cinematic self-consciousness.

10. MIDGE AND CARLOTTA

Midge's apartment is the scene immediately following the kissing on the beach (which ended with Madeleine pleading, "Stay with me," and Scottie whispering back, "Always"). We see Midge now in a red sweater. (We are becoming used to the idea of red as, to simplify crudely, a marker of passion, or a passionately charged environment,[90] just as we are becoming used to the idea of green as a color of mystery and the past, so red is an unusual color for Midge, given what we have been led to believe about her.) She is facing stage left now, not right as before, and is standing, not sitting, and is at an upright easel, illuminated by a strong light, and is painting something of her own, not designing ad copy for underwear, chuckling to herself, when Scottie arrives. She hides the museum brochure she has been using as her model. (She has obviously been to the Palace of Fine Arts and has seen the painting.)

We do not know, or at least did not see, what happened in between Madeleine and Scottie's kiss and this evening arrival. If they left for the sequoias in the morning, and kissed passionately soon after they arrived, a good deal of time has elapsed. We certainly do not see Madeleine drop Scottie off at his apartment and say good-bye, and the kiss was romantic (über-romantic, as discussed), passionate, and intimate. Especially given the last words we hear between them, it is safe to assume that they arrived later at that "somewhere," making love, beginning an affair, that Madeleine mentioned when she found a way to tell Scottie what was going to happen if he got into her car. So we have to imagine that experience having had a profound, very recent effect on him, given how much he has emphasized the solitary quality of his life up until then.

So it is not entirely fair to say that Midge simply, and somewhat typically, "misunderstood" Scottie, when she badly underestimated the ef-

90. As is the dining room at Ernie's, and, it turns out, the first scene in Scottie's apartment when Madeleine is wearing the red robe. Hitchcock is so attentive to these issues and especially to these complementary colors that almost every scene involves some variation on their relation. Madeleine's green Jaguar parked outside Scottie's red door, or the choice of gray for the color of both Midge's sports car and Madeleine's signature suit. See Friedlander, "Being-in-(Techni)Color," for a commentary on the most important instances.

fect of her comic picture. After all, the Scottie she knew was the one who breezily scoffed at Elster's suggestion of ghostly possession and whose lighthearted unseriousness strayed into thoughtlessness and cruelty. But now, after the beginning of his affair with Madeleine, he is somber and unresponsive to her queries, perhaps feeling slightly guilty at hiding what he has done from his old friend and ex-fiancée. He is certainly a changed man from the one we saw in the opening scene in Midge's apartment.

Here we might pause to note that the stress throughout on the implications and dimensions of unknowingness and persistent opacity in Hitchcock's world does not imply that this unknowingness is always momentous and of great philosophical significance. There is plenty of ordinary misunderstanding everywhere in the films too, and this is an instance. There is no reason for Midge to have imagined or anticipated why Scottie would be different from the man we saw in the first apartment scene, the flip, boyish, emotionally closed and prickly fellow we first knew. And there is no suggestion, as there often is in Hitchcock, that there are strong "internal" reasons, her own desires and needs, that prevent her from seeing what she otherwise could, that she "prevents herself" from seeing them.[91] But the consequences of her not being, not being able to be, "up" on what has been happening to Scottie are shocking to her, and momentous for their relationship. But all of that results from simple human finitude; our inability often to know what we need to know in a temporally fluid, changing existence in order to relate to others in ways we can understand and manage.

He enters the apartment irritated that she has left a note under his door (no doubt while he was out with Madeleine),[92] one he finds suffused, he says, with a hint of "desperation." He is brusque and a bit rude as she finds several ways to ask him what he has been up to, to which he keeps responding, with growing impatience, simply "wandering," with all the meaning that term has come to have. (He might as well say, "I have been yearning.") However changed, though, he is still capable of his usual

---

91. One of Hitchcock's best treatments of when and how these factors do motivate a kind of willful ignorance is *Notorious*. In this case, Midge no doubt has her own reasons for wanting to see only the old Johnny, but things have moved too fast in the present case for even those to be relevant.

92. Was she watching the apartment again, resolved to act when she saw them leave together, or did she simply find him gone when she arrived?

insensitivity. When she says she has gone back to her first love, painting, he notes tactlessly that he always thought she was wasting her talents "in the underwear department." She has to remind him that "it's a living," in effect, that people have to work, not all of them are "fairly independent." She offers to show him the painting and he walks over to it. There he sees the museum portrait of Carlotta, although instead of Carlotta's head, Midge has painted her own (figure 16). When Scottie sees the painting, he shakes his head sadly and says simply no and repeats twice, "That's not funny, Midge." He says this while we see a frame that pairs the painting on the right with Midge sitting on the left in exactly the same pose, a look of great concern on her face, as she realizes from his look that she has made a terrible mistake (figure 17).

The shot showing the identity of the poses of Midge and the painted Carlotta/Midge has a great deal of pathos. She has literally tried to paint herself into his sight, his regard, by painting her face on Carlotta's body in the portrait Madeleine visits, another attempt to make an exterior mean what one wants it to mean. She is suggesting to him that they both, at bottom, realize that the Carlotta fantasy is comic—a serious miscalculation on her part—and she theatricalizes herself; in a way she pledges by this act (half-ironically) to be whoever will attract Scottie. She no doubt expects the same response that she got recently, in the car, when he insisted he is only reporting what Elster believes, not what he believes, still insisting (pretending a bit) that he is not intrigued by all this this mumbo jumbo. Her gesture means to say, playfully, if it is haunted women you want, well, I'll be one. It is her attempt to be part of the "plot," the other plot, the one she is shut out of, that creates the pathos, captured by her even posing as Carlotta, all for him, but he is no longer the Scottie she could reliably count on, and a passion has been stirred in him that Midge seems to know she will never be able to excite in him. She is also playfully suggesting by the painting that it is possible for Scottie to have the exoticism and mystery of the "Carlotta" side of the feminine joined together with the realistic, prudent, sensible domestic side. (As in so many other aspects of the film, here too the suggestion is that one person can be two or more personae. Or, at least in this case, one can imagine playing both roles, embodying the mysterious sexual aura of Madeleine/Carlotta and the sensible side of love,

FIG. 16

FIG. 17

both maternal and companionate/marital. The painting is a reminder that some people just can't successfully play all the roles they want and need to play.) She realizes in a flash that her attempt to caricature the Madeleine plot has failed badly, and she realizes that she may have even lost his friendship, and castigates herself, trying to deface the painting, hurling an

FIG. 18

instrument at her reflection in the window and grabbing and pulling her hair, while she recriminates herself (figure 18).[93]

11. THE "SUICIDE"

The film cuts from Scottie's departure to him wandering the streets of San Francisco, very likely all night. No doubt, Hitchcock includes these few seconds to emphasize how deeply Scottie has been affected, how upended his world now is. The camera then cuts to him in his apartment. He is still in the same clothes, dozing on his couch, when the doorbell rings and Madeleine arrives.

She tells him she has had the dream again, the one with the tower and her being "pulled into the darkness," although this time she is full of a

93. Throughout the film, reflections in mirrors and windows highlight the duality of appearance or reflection and original, as well as the link between that image and the various personae one person can publicly present. One is always at least two. In her attack on her reflection, she is castigating herself for playing the wrong "Midge": the sarcastic, ironic, rational old-pal Midge, but it seems to be the only role Scottie will let her play.

wealth of details, enough, presumably, to make it possible for Scottie to recognize the tower as a real place, the San Juan Bautista mission. How Elster knows that Scottie knows of this mission, and why he thinks he can count on Scottie wanting to take her there, and right away, later that day, just on the day when he breaks his wife's neck in anticipation of the fake suicide, are among the nearly endless improbabilities of the murder plan. But, as throughout, Hitchcock seems more liberated from conventions of Hollywood film narrative than he does in any other film, and when he has Judy relate the plan to us, as she writes a letter to Scottie confessing (which she tears up), he does not bother to try to sort any of this out.[94]

But Scottie is indeed hooked, and very excited that she "has given him something to work with." He is convinced in some way he does not explain that if he can show her that the site of her dream is a real place, she will believe that she has been there before, that that is how she knows all the details, and she will then be cured, will not be able to continue to believe she is haunted, possessed, by a dead Carlotta. (This is rather like telling a depressed person that she has no good reason to be depressed, and insisting that when she realizes that, she will stop being depressed.) He does not reckon that this might be a dangerous gamble, that if Madeleine

---

94. The film has been called the first mainstream Hollywood surrealist film, and given all the improbabilities, that is understandable. How does Elster know Scottie will be so smitten by Madeleine? How does he know that Scottie, especially after what he says in Elster's office, will not, after the jump in the bay, insist that Madeleine is mentally ill and requires immediate psychiatric intervention? What is to stop Scottie from investigating more thoroughly the Carlotta story (as a trained detective would) and discovering that there is no connection to the Elsters, that what Elster told him in the club is all false? For that matter, what is to stop Scottie from interrogating third parties about Madeleine and discovering that she is not in town? How can he so confidently count on Scottie not being able to get up those stairs in the tower, be so sure that his passion for Madeleine will not overcome the disability? (He almost does make it to the top, in fact.) How did Elster manage to haul his wife's body up all those flights of stairs without being seen? We learn later that there are apparently nuns traipsing through the bell tower all the time. (In the opening pan of the mission grounds, we see a nun out and about.) How can he count on Scottie being so stunned that he leaves the scene of the fake suicide, does not attend to the corpse for one last look at his beloved and discover that the dead blonde is not his Madeleine? As noted, these questions are endless, and the question they raise is whether Hitchcock has created a context, even a kind of fantasy or dream context, so compelling in itself, so focused on the dynamics of fantasy and love, that the viewer cares as little about such plot details as the viewer does about whether time travel is really possible as depicted in science fiction, or whether there can really be angels who intervene in a depressed man's life, and so on.

continues to believe that she has not been there, and it remains plausible that this could be the village "to the south" that Pop Leibel said was Carlotta's home[95] (perhaps she was educated in the convent school, which Madeleine-as-Carlotta pretends to remember later, and began to sing and dance in the saloon that Scottie mentions), then the credibility of the Carlotta haunting could be *enhanced*, and Madeleine could slip further into despair. Moreover, it is of a piece with the view Scottie has about how to "cure" great psychological distress and turmoil that became apparent in the step stool cure for vertigo he proposed at the outset. Given that the Carlotta story is also intertwined with Hitchcock's treatment of such issues as the role of fantasy in romantic love, the often irrational burden of the past on the present, its inescapability and haunting presence, and the potentially destructive consequences (yet unavoidability) of the whole mythology of romantic love, the weakness of Scottie's rational approach to such issues, even as he is in the grip of an obsession, the full power of which he will only fully appreciate when he thinks Madeleine has committed suicide, is all clearly a comment on the rational, skeptical attitude of some viewers, their confidence that *they* would never be subject to such turmoil, that there is always a rational explanation for all such phenomena.

On a first viewing, we are certainly invited to think that the film is portraying the ghost/haunting plot as credible in the world of the movie, although we think ourselves insulated from that belief, and by taking Scottie as credible, we are invited to be suspicious, to suspect neurosis, even as we remain uncertain what the film is inviting us to believe.[96] When it turns out to be neither a haunting nor a neurosis, we are exactly in Scottie's final position, made to feel a bit foolish—a clear sentiment of many first reviewers, palpably angry at being duped—but, if we have been caught up in the film at all, also unwilling to "lose faith" in the two characters, even as Scottie, after learning the truth, can still, with great passion and visible love, call Judy by the name of someone he knows never existed. The strange truth this seems to embody is the fact that having an illusion revealed does not necessarily destroy it, any more than telling ourselves at a film that is creat-

95.   San Juan Bautista is in fact ninety-one miles to the south of San Francisco.

96.   We are thus in much the same position as Henry James's readers in *Turn of the Screw* (1898). In that story, though, we are left forever suspended.

ing great tension or sadness that "it is only a movie" eradicates the tension or sadness.

On the drive out, Hitchcock films them sitting quietly in the front seat of Madeleine's car, with no dialogue. In some scenes, such as the red bathrobe scene in Scottie's apartment and this one, Kim Novak looks every bit as young as the twenty-four she was when the movie was made, an endearing trait, if, on subsequent viewings, we appreciate that as a very young, naïve Kansas girl, she has gotten herself into something she now dearly wishes to get out of. We are asked to consider (at least once we have seen the film a first time) what she must be thinking as they drive out, since a great deal seems to be going through her mind. Her eyes keep darting to and fro, and she seems pensive and apprehensive (figure 19). We see, from her point of view, the open blue sky above them, and perhaps this is a way of showing us that she might be trying to imagine a way out of the situation she has made for herself, especially if we believe that she has truly fallen in love with Scottie. This will be her insistence in the later, parallel scene at the mission, after Scottie has guessed the truth, and once we know that she claims her love to be and to have been true, we must watch the film again, looking for signs of this early love and any sign of reluctance to carry out the plan. After all, this, that she loved Scottie and wanted to get out of the plan, is what she *would* say upon being discovered. More on

FIG. 19

that later. The point now is that if there were to be a time to confess and ask Scottie for help in protecting her from the consequences, this would be it. And she does not, open blue sky above her and all.

After a pan of the mission grounds, we see Madeleine in the stables, seated on a buggy, with Scottie standing next to her. "It's all real!"[97] he tells Madeleine and implores her to try to remember when she was really there. Madeleine goes into full Carlotta mode, vacant expression and all, remembering, but as Carlotta, obviously still fully committed to the plan and in no visible discomfort. The more details she remembers, the more enthusiastically Scottie points out as evidence that she knows details so well that she must have been there as Madeleine, apparently not realizing that all such "evidence" could just as easily prove the credibility of Madeleine's "possession." Yes, there is a gray horse in the livery, but it is stuffed, something consistent with the "real" memory of Carlotta, of what happened in her past. His "You see, there's an answer for everything" begins to sound not just overly optimistic, but pathetic. He begs her to try hard to remember when she was here as Madeleine. She gets off the buggy still in a Carlotta daze, and they embrace and kiss. (The Madeleine musical theme begins again, so we know that she is back to being Madeleine.) In a gesture that will recur later, Madeleine's eyes look away toward the tower (faintly resonant with the unknown woman's darting eyes in the credits), and the decisive fake suicide begins.[98] She whispers, "It's too late," just as Scottie will later, meaning something quite different with the same words (plate 15).

She turns and runs toward the tower. Scottie catches her and turns her to him, and now we do see Madeleine's clear distress and hear her complain that what is happening is not "fair," that "it wasn't supposed to happen this way." He clutches her and the Madeleine musical theme begins again. She asks him if he believes she loves him, and says, "And if you lose me, you'll know I loved you and wanted to go on loving you." She begins to run toward the tower, and it dawns on Scottie what might be happening, another suicide attempt. He rushes to catch up, but she has a head start and he must confront those stairs. Twice we see from his point of view down

97. A phrase replete with Hitchcockian irony. Nothing is real, least of all Madeleine.
98. The second time, while kissing Scottie, she sees over his shoulder some spectral figure coming up and toward them, and steps back in fright and falls.

FIG. 20

the stairwell, and twice we see the reverse zoom that signals his vertigo, and he pauses. He has managed to get fairly high, but those two pauses have cost him dearly, and he hears a scream, and looks out the window in horror as the body of a blonde woman in a gray suit falls by (plate 16).

Obviously falling apart emotionally, he descends slowly down the stairs as a priest, workers, and nuns are climbing a ladder up to the body, which has landed on a lower level of the roof. Hitchcock switches to a very high angle shot, from no one's point of view. The scene is stark and the tonality has a mysterious air, rather like a de Chirico painting.[99] Given the height of the camera position (we have seen no structure higher than the tower, so that position is outside the world of the movie), much higher than the height that stopped Scottie, a contrast seems implied. We the viewers, and Hitchcock, it would appear, do not have a problem, Scottie's problem, with height, acrophobia, and vertigo. We are able to see, nonvertiginously, Scottie, a tiny figure from this height, walk away toward the right (figure 20). His not remaining at the suicide will have to be explained later.

On a first viewing, we are stunned that the female lead of the movie has died, and in such a senseless way, and experience great sympathy for Scottie, who could not *be rescued* before because of his vertigo, and now could

99. For example, see Giorgio de Chirico's *The Nostalgia for the Infinite*.

not *rescue* the woman who is the love of his life because of the same disastrous limitation. And we are confused by the pace of the movie. Barely an hour and twenty minutes have passed. Is the movie about to end? It is almost long enough; it could end. Will there just be one final wrap-up, and *this* is the story? A man falls in love with a disturbed woman and she jumps from a tower in front of his horrified eyes? The End?

This dual aspect of the implications of Scottie's vertigo—a man dies trying to help him, and he cannot help a woman who jumps to her death—continues to suggest something about the state of his emotional life, especially his relations of independence and dependence, active and passive, with respect to others (being able to help and being able to be helped), and that is starting to bring the nonliteral and more general meaning of his vertigo into focus. Something seems to be preventing him from fully receiving or giving help. As noted in the introduction, somehow working out a practical, healthy balance between the ideal of independence (nonconformism, authenticity, feeling that one's life is one's own) and the fact of, and need for, dependence, especially the need for respect, appreciation, esteem, and above all love, is in itself already a task that one could describe as vertiginous, dizzying in its complexity. A particularly closed-off individual, opaque to himself and insensitive to these complexities, someone like Scottie, might be expected to suffer from very serious vertigo in the larger sense. In the midst of passionate romantic love, this limitation and so disability can be so intense as to be calamitous. One can end up "frozen," unable to go further "up," and barely able to come back down, afraid of one's own putative claim to independence, and afraid of the implications of acknowledging one's dependence. It can even provoke, without the person being aware of it, that dialectical fear of falling I mentioned earlier: the fear of letting go, of wanting death as an escape from such paralysis. (When someone is manipulating this condition common to all humanity—love, the need for love, and so the susceptibility to deception, self-deception, fantasy, wishful thinking, all because of love's intensity—for his or her own ends, one has zero chance of working any of this out. It is doubly calamitous.) The high, potentially dizzying shot of the bell tower and of Scottie's smallness as he sneaks away suggests it is possible to tolerate the threat of such vertigo without succumbing to it, although, as ever with

Hitchcock, taking that possibility for granted would be a bad mistake. We are about to see a warning to that effect.

12. THE CORONER'S INQUEST

A sign of Hitchcock's attentiveness to these issues is his more general warning, as it were, that a straightforward contrast among the three categories I have been discussing—deceit, fantasy, and the (putative) plain, unvarnished truth—would be simplistic. We have an example of the latter—a simplistic belief in access to the unvarnished truth and a supreme confidence in moral evaluation—at the coroner's inquest, which for some reason is being held on the mission grounds. The opening pan in the first shot after the camera cuts from the fake suicide is completely identical to the opening pan shown when we first saw the mission, although now it is filled with cars and police. It is some sign, perhaps, that everything has changed, that "the mission," while it is the same place, has acquired a completely different meaning, especially for Scottie, but also for us. We still think we know what that changed meaning is, but we are, and will come to know that we are, wrong. The truth about "the mission," about what happened there, how it should be remembered, is known by only two persons at this point, Elster, who is there at the inquest, and Judy Barton.

Nothing the grotesquely self-satisfied, smug coroner (played brilliantly by the veteran character actor, Henry Jones [figure 21]) says is false. He lays out clearly what appears to be true, what can be said to be true by a "disinterested" observer.[100] It was manifestly foolish of Elster to entrust his

---

100. The difficulty of understanding each other from such a perspective (as an observer, from the "outside") is treated with the complexity it warrants in *Rear Window*, the story of a photographer who photographs spectacle and war ("outsides"), and who, laid up with a broken leg, spies on his neighbors and thinks he has them all figured out, down to summary clichés for all of them: "Miss Lonely Hearts," "Miss Torso," and, he begins to think, even "Wife Murderer." This is also an obvious warning about how much viewers of a movie can expect to understand simply by observing, watching, apart from what the director calls attention to, apart from their own efforts and engagement. In the Hitchcock cameo in the film, Hitchcock has turned toward a pianist in one of the apartments, but

FIG. 21

increasingly insane wife's well-being not to a professional but to a retired detective with a disability, vertigo. Scottie did have a "weakness" that made it impossible for him to help when "he was most needed." But the fatuous coroner also misses everything "emotionally" true about the bond between Scottie and Madeleine (an emotional bond we can also call "being bound up in overlapping fantasies"), misses the vulnerability of each that follows from such a fantastical romance, and, of course, misses the "fact" of the murderer sitting right in front of him, and everything else about the Elster plot.[101] But what is most important is that everything he says is also charged with a moralistic certainty, a self-satisfied confidence in making a string of moral evaluations about Scottie's "irresponsibilities." It is almost always the case in Hitchcock's films that any character who claims

---

he appears to be looking straight at us, the viewer, as if to say, "Pay attention." The same kind of gesture occurs in his cameo in *Marnie*. It is only when Lisa (Grace Kelly) climbs through the murderer's window, as if climbing into a movie screen (Buster Keaton's *Sherlock, Jr.* [1924] seems invoked) that the reality of the murder can be established, that is, only when observation becomes direct engagement.

101.   More implausibilities arise, and are ignored. It was presumably possible in 1958 for an autopsy to show whether the real Mrs. Elster's neck was broken before the fall or from the fall. I raise all of these merely to suggest that within the dynamic of the film, they don't matter. We pass over them effortlessly. At least most viewers captured by the film would. I concede that there may be many who find the murder plan a barrier to being so captured.

to know what's going on, and especially to evince great confidence in his or her moral judgments, is being mocked in some way, treated ironically, sometimes, as here, even with clear Hitchcockian contempt.[102] It is the interplay of these three categories, and the difficulty of separating them, that appears to make any straightforward moral reaction to the events difficult. (It is almost as if Hitchcock is signaling to any viewer who misses a moral dimension in the movie thus far that, if that is what he wants, *here* is what it looks like.)

After the jury confers for ten seconds and rules the death a suicide, Elster pulls Scottie aside and explains that he is leaving the country, and he apologizes for getting Scottie involved. He tries to shake Scottie's hand, but Scottie does not offer his, not, apparently, in rejection. He seems too numb, crushed by what has happened, and gives the impression that he barely understands what is happening. (He does not speak at any point at the inquest.) But his reluctance to shake Elster's hand might signal the *tiniest* bit of unformed, slowly dawning realization by Scottie, the professional detective, an insight he somehow does not yet know he has. For Elster says, "There's no way for them to understand. You and I know who killed Madeleine." On a second viewing, we get the irony. That person is not Carlotta but Elster, and his remark hints at the possibility that Scottie may know the truth without fully knowing that he knows. After we see the dream sequence, perhaps we will suspect even more strongly that something in all of this is not sitting well with Scottie.

So let us take stock (as all these factors are about to get exponentially more convoluted): the complications we have seen in self- and other-understanding, the unavoidable ones, stem from the inevitable distortions that must result from a number of factors—simple human finitude for one, and the limitations that come with such finitude. For another, there is often the subject's *desire* to be seen a certain way, and a desire to see the other in a certain way, the latter potentially causing an unavoidable distortion in the former. There have been several examples: what Midge

---

102.   Horowitz, in "Made-to-Order Witness," rightly points out that this is also true for psychoanalytic claims to authoritative knowledge, something the films themselves seem to invite. Such claims to insight, as Freud clearly recognized, can be diversions, screens, false leads, self-interested and self-deceived, and the like.

wants to see in her Johnny, what Johnny refuses to see in Midge, what Scottie hopes to be true about Madeleine. As noted before, even in what seem harmless cases, like wanting to be seen in one's "best light," complications arise about what one is thereby in effect hiding, and about the source of one's conception of "one's best light." And the other's look is also inevitably entangled in a desire to see the other subject in a certain way, a desire complexly prompted by the other's self-image, projected in a way that might not coincide with how one might want to see the other. The dynamic of love makes it especially difficult, impossible, to separate what "shows up" for one in one's regard of the beloved, and one's intense desire to be loved by the object of one's love. This is what, I have been suggesting, is truly vertiginous, this unstable dynamic of love, that most intense figure for all human relationships of dependence between independent beings. To insist on certainty, tests, proof, "the truth," all to protect oneself from "falling," being hurt, might cure one of such vertigo, but it lands one in the same position as Scottie in the last frame, cured but alone.

Herein lies the link between the film and the Orpheus myth, something occasionally noted by commentators. Orpheus has a "second chance" with Eurydice, but is instructed that he cannot look back at her as they leave the underworld. He does and he loses her a second time. In many interpretations, he looks back because he cannot believe that what he had been told is correct; he is afraid that she will not be safely following him. As we will see later, Scottie's forcing Judy up the stairs in the film's finale, the proximate cause of his losing her a second time, has the same air of skepticism, as does his insistence on seeing Judy as she "really is" (as if there is such a thing), his refusal to accept that he *has* found *her*, has found his "Madeleine." Like Orpheus's inability to believe that he has rescued his beloved from the dead, Scottie's need to believe his fantasy (that Madeleine is another person altogether), not what he can see to be true,[103] ensures that she will remain dead.

What we will see later in the film, Scottie's attempt to remake Judy as Madeleine, is only an extremely dramatic, spectacularly futile attempt to see what one wants to see, but that is an ineliminable feature of romantic

---

103. For me, at any rate, the most heartrending line in the film is Scottie's address to Judy after he has learned all the facts, the truth that Madeleine was never Madeleine, but always Judy: "I loved you so, *Madeleine.*"

(and all significant) relationships. And just because one wants to see what one needs to see so desperately, there can be nothing valuable or finally satisfying to see. Once Scottie succeeds, he fails; once Judy has been made into Madeleine, it is ever clearer who *Judy* is, not who he wants her to be (a "real" Madeleine, a fantasy). That is, it is inevitable that he will also see how it could be possible for her to become Madeleine, inevitable that he will see the real, deceptive Judy, as well as, in a way we need to explore, the real Madeleine that is in Judy, the product of her ability to be Madeleine as easily as she is Judy.

In general, there are many such things that one might want, but in *trying* to get them, one makes their achievement impossible. Trying to do what will bring you a good reputation results in a worthless reputation, an artificial one, since you are truly honored for what you genuinely do, not for what you do *in order to be well regarded*. Trying to make another love you by being whomever it is you think the other would love, or trying to make another into someone whom you can love, obeys the same self-defeating logic. And in the same sense, trying to make a fantasy real is subject to the same self-undermining dynamic. It can't be *real* if you, the maker, always know it is artificial, made by you. It can fool everyone else but you. One aspect of the powerful impact the movie has had on so many people has to do with the fact that, despite these limitations and dangers, Scottie's attempt embodies something we recognize as a living ambition in all of us, regardless of the rational limitations of the project. What a miserable thing "reality" would be if there were no hope that our fantasies could find some footing in the real.

Thus, when he succeeds in remaking Madeleine, he loses her again; even loses his loss, cannot even mourn the original Madeleine since he did not lose Madeleine. Judy's Madeleine was a fiction, a fantasy. Further, all the social relationships we observe in the film feature a complex dynamic that involves some mode of self-presentation and some mode of being represented by another, and this involves some acknowledgment of one's dependence on the other, and some insistence on one's independence in such dependence. I said before that Scottie might be wary of Midge because she knows (and he suspects she knows) that he is not as independent as he seems (perhaps that he is still a boy, a big boy, but a boy). And perhaps she knows this from the way their engagement was broken off. This would suggest that Scottie lives alone because he cannot respond to any acknowledgment of dependence and has his own anxiety about his self-asserted independence.

All of this has a great deal to do with the dynamics of cinema too, with what a director wants us to see and especially not see, but also with what he wants those who love the film to see, those who are "equal" to the film, up to it, as if some element of Hitchcock cinema is more like courtship than seduction, not at all just his infamous manipulation. At least this or any film can be such an invitation to those who might love the film, at least if the film is not an assault on the viewer, a denial of the separation between the outside film world and the inside mental world of the spectator. The historical world described in the introduction has a bearing on the artist-audience relationship, since that too is a social relationship, and it is one that Hitchcock is constantly thematizing, especially in *Vertigo*.[104]

As originally suggested, all of this makes the question of power and freedom unavoidable. In fact, such a fluid and unstable dynamic can appear to be, and has so appeared to philosophers like Sartre, fundamentally threatening and always fraught with an unresolvable anxiety.[105] For Sartre, it would seem that just being regarded is implicitly always objectifying and tinged with a shame at being regarded in a way one cannot control, at being taken so easily to be an object for a subject. But that does no justice to a certain tragic element in the dynamic struggle to see and be seen in a way that is finally satisfying to both, a genuine quest to see and be seen *as each is*, the achievement of some genuine mutuality, each being seen as also seeing.[106] Being regarded by another often involves the genuine attempt

---

104.   The best study I have come across of the different ways one might think of the Hitchcockian understanding of the relation between the spectator and the film is Andrew Klevan's "*Vertigo* and the Spectator of Film Analysis," in Makkai, *Vertigo*, 194–224. For more on the sociality theme and its relevance to modernist art, see Pippin, *After the Beautiful*.

105.   The bearing of Sartre on all of this is suggested by Katalin Makkai in her thoughtful essay "*Vertigo* and Being Seen," in Makkai, *Vertigo*, 139–73. What follows in this paragraph is my disagreement with the particular use she makes of Sartre (I rely much more on Sartre's source here, the 1807 Hegel). I stress that the disagreement is with the use of Sartre for *Vertigo*. Her account of what a Sartrian view of *Vertigo* amounts to is quite right, but such a view misses a good deal of the pathos and tragedy of the film, and Sartre's account of these struggles has always seemed to me strangely moralistic, something the film certainly is not.

106.   For Sartre, of course, there is no such thing as "who one really is." That would be a confusion of *en-soi* and *pour-soi*, and claiming that about oneself is a paradigmatic example of what happens

by the other to see another *as a subject*. Especially in romantic relations, something is going *wrong* if "the look," to use Sartre's famous phrase, is inherently objectifying. It can hardly be said to be the fate of looking and being looked at in itself. That is why the Judy-makeover-by-Scottie we are about to discuss is so creepy.[107] From his point of view, Scottie is not "objectifying" Judy or treating her as a means, because he is asking her to alter only trivial details in her appearance; that is, he is only trying to release the "subject Madeleine" perhaps hidden within. But his obsessive need to do so is already an indication that the relation between inside and outside is far more complicated, far less separable, than any simple invocation of "subjective" and "objective" categories would allow.[108]

13. SCOTTIE'S DREAM

After the inquest, there is one scene of Scottie, shot from below, visiting Madeleine's new grave, with open blue sky above him. It is a very brief

---

in bad faith. It is this nondialectical opposition that limits Sartre's understanding of the look. By contrast, cf. Hegel's remarks in his chapter on self-consciousness: "A *self-consciousness* exists *for a self-consciousness*. Only thereby does self-consciousness in fact exist, for it is only therein that the unity of itself in its otherness comes to be for it. The *I*, which is the object of its concept, is in fact not an *object*. However, the object of desire is merely *self-sufficient*, for it is the universal, indestructible substance, the fluid essence in-parity-with-itself. Because a self-consciousness is the object, the object is just as much an I as it is an object. — The concept *of spirit* is thereby on hand for us." G. W. F. Hegel, *Phänomenologie des Geistes*, trans. Terry Pinkard, § 177, http://terrypinkard.weebly.com/phenomenology-of-spirit-page.html (last updated October 30, 2013).

107. Hitchcock suggests that what Scottie is doing by dressing Judy as Madeleine is undressing Judy as Judy, much as he had done before, and that when she emerges from the bathroom as Madeleine, she is, in effect, Judy nude. See François Truffaut, *Hitchcock*, rev. ed. (New York: Simon and Schuster, 1985), 244.

108. I have been referring throughout to the interplay between romantic love, with its elements of irrationality (as self-opacity) and chance, and obsession. One could put the relation as it is presented in the film in one of two ways: either that Hitchcock believes that romantic love necessarily and dangerously involves an irrational obsessive attachment or that he wants us to see the potential in romantic love to become neurotically obsessional. I think that he is suggesting the former, but exploring this further would require a much longer discussion. (The same issue arises in film noir in the relation between the femme fatale and the smitten protagonist. See Pippin, *Fatalism in American Film Noir*.) I am grateful to Mark Jenkins and Paul Kottman for correspondence about this issue.

scene, only sixteen seconds or so, and the camera cuts immediately to him in bed, tossing and turning. Since the grave scene is in effect the beginning of his post-Madeleine existence, it seems to connect more with what follows it, the dream, than what precedes it, and thereby, on retrospect, given what we will now see, it could be thought of as a kind of prologue to the dream, as if Scottie has come to the grave to ask something: what really happened? And the dream *is* that interrogation. As we watch, the camera moves in on his head tossing back and forth, and various colors, blue, a reddish blue or pink, and a purple, flash on the screen. Then, in another remarkable sign that the dream is more like an active interrogation than something that befalls him, *Scottie opens his eyes.* His dream begins, and he continues "dreaming" with his eyes open. It has eight sequences: an animated cartoon image of Madeleine's bouquet of flowers, coming apart into bits; a memory shot of Elster and Scottie standing by the window at the inquest, although now Carlotta Valdez herself, dressed as she was in her portrait, is standing between them, close to Elster; a shot of the portrait and a close-up of the necklace that will play such a revelatory role later;[109] a shot of Scottie walking in a cemetery, red lights flashing; a shot of him reaching the open grave of Carlotta Valdez, with the camera descending down into its darkness; a shot of his head detached from his body, as if hurtling through space, wind blowing his hair, against a graphic background of what appears to be some weblike design; a shot of his body, or a kind of cutout of his body, in silhouette, falling toward the red-tile lower roof where Madeleine fell; and finally, in the last shot, the roof disappears and we just see the silhouette falling in open space.

I am far from understanding everything Hitchcock is trying to accomplish by filming this dream, but there seems to be an underlying thematic, or at least I would like to suggest one. The beginning flashing lights, before the dream proper starts, clearly signal Scottie's emotional turmoil, perhaps a range of emotions, guilt, sadness, despair, confusion, as he tries to sleep. The first image, the cartoon of the bouquet, is a return to the very first link between Madeleine and Carlotta. (She has the small bouquet made as an exact replica of the one Carlotta holds in the portrait, and Scottie sees her

---

109.   If nothing else, the lingering shot of the necklace establishes for the viewer that Scottie has noticed it; it is lodged securely in his memory.

buy it after entering the flower shop in a strange, secretive way.) Perhaps, as Robin Wood has suggested, the obvious artificiality of the cartoon is quite deliberate on Hitchcock's part, and is meant to suggest to us the artificiality or even staged nature of this purported link with Carlotta. Perhaps it even represents Scottie's impression of the link and its artificiality, the first moment of the thematic I want to suggest. The flowers disintegrating suggest Madeleine's actions in tearing the bouquet into bits, and if the link itself is artificial, "drawn" by someone rather than real, perhaps this pre-suicide action was also staged, was an artifice.[110]

The scene of the window conversation at the inquest adds Carlotta to the memory, but Carlotta is, oddly, not centrally located but standing by Elster, as if they belong together on one side, Scottie on the other. This is the scene where Elster says, "You and I both know who killed Madeleine." Scottie does not dream about Carlotta alone, but linked with Elster, and not with Madeleine. In general, it is also interesting that while this is a nightmare tied to the suicide, Scottie is not dreaming of Madeleine falling, of her corpse, of the last moments in the tower, of her turning into Carlotta, of her looking up and beseeching him as she falls, and so forth. Madeleine is not in the dream. It is not much of a stretch to say he (or "his unconscious") is trying to work something out in the dream, going over elements from the Carlotta-Elster-Madeleine links, rather than dreaming in a way that could be said to show great guilt and pain, or even to be "about" the suicide itself, the trauma.

Next, Scottie is walking purposively, first against a black backdrop and then a cemetery materializes behind him. Then we see him finding and peering into the empty grave of Carlotta. What is unusual about the scene (and very easy to miss on a first viewing) is Scottie's expression. It is not pained or shocked. He is *puzzled*. His brows are furrowed and he is clearly pursuing some sort of question (figure 22).

When he gets to Carlotta's grave, it is empty. Where is Carlotta if not dead and in her grave? She can't be out haunting Madeleine if Madeleine is also dead. Is it a sign that there is and was no Carlotta, at least no Carlotta who possessed Madeleine and drove her to suicide? As the camera and presumably Scottie plunge into the black depths of the grave, Scottie's

110. Wood, *Hitchcock's Films Revisited*, 117.

FIG. 22

head appears as if hurtling forward, colors flashing, projected against a weblike graphic (the web he begins to suspect snared him?). Again, the most striking thing is that there is no look of fear or anxiety on his face, but puzzlement (figure 23). Is the speed here suggesting the speed of the growing and accumulating doubt that all was not as it seemed with the suicide?[111]

Then something frightening does occur: his silhouette falls onto the mission roof, and then falls in free, empty space (figure 24). What is so striking about this is that he is not dreaming of the victim falling (Madeleine) but of *himself* falling. (It is useful to remember that Scottie had early on mentioned to Midge that he *did* regularly dream of the policeman falling.) This may be connected with the fear of falling/desire to fall I mentioned before, but in this case his dream logic has transposed victims! Now he is dreaming as if *he* were the falling victim,[112] or at least the one "this is all about," and in silhouette because his role, what it all *does* have to do with him, is not "filled in" yet. And perhaps the issue is not just his inability to save Madeleine, but his fall is a plunge into something that is thus far blank,

---

111. I am grateful to Lisa Van Alstyne for conversations about Scottie's dream.

112. When Judy writes her confessional note later, she tells him explicitly, "You were the victim. I was the tool, and you were the victim."

FIG. 23

FIG. 24

unlocatable, beyond the particular setting of her death. It is thus telling that when he wakes up in a fright, he seems to be frightened by something *from* the dream, not by just having had the dream, as if he has seen something but does not yet know what it is, does not yet see why all of this does not fit together, and is frightened by that (figure 25). (It is a dream because he knows or suspects something he cannot quite bring to consciousness,

FIG. 25

but there is a definite sense in the sequence that he is in effect "going over evidence"; his detective brain is working.)

14. MUSIC THERAPY

The film cuts to the front of a hospital where Midge's gray sports car is parked outside, and the camera takes us inside to the room where Scottie is a patient. He in some sort of acute catatonic state, unresponsive to anything going on around him. Midge is present and has brought along some Mozart, having heard from the nurses there that music therapy is possible. She jokes around about music for other kinds of mental illnesses and what would happen if the wrong sort of music was played for a patient. Not only is this a reminder of Midge's difficulty understanding Scottie (she has brought the same kind of music that he made clear he did not like in the opening scene in her apartment); it also makes clear that her attempts to help are so ineffective as to border on the pathetic.[113] She pleads with him

---

113.   It is also possible that Hitchcock wants to point to the similarity between this attempt with music and Scottie's various attempts to master the irrational and unknown, something where Midge

FIG. 26

to "try." Try what? Try to be sane, to "pull himself out of this"? She tells him that he is not lost, that "mother is here," again recalling the first apartment scene and his first sharp words to her, "Don't be so motherly," that is, exactly what she is now trying to be. In a conversation with his doctor, she learns that it may take six months to a year for him to recover (we later learn that he is out of commission for a year) and that he is not participating in his own recovery, and he is not talking. Midge tells the doctor that he was in love with Madeleine and that he still is, and, finally admitting to herself the enormity of the change that this love has wrought in her Johnny, she remarks that Mozart is not going to help at all. That is, she seems to have realized that she is no longer part of Johnny's life, no longer can be, and her slow, painful walk down the corridor signals as much that she is leaving the hospital as that she is conceding defeat and leaving his life (figure 26).[114]

_____

could expect to find some common ground with the sensible Scot of the first part of the film. But, in the language the film is teaching us to learn, Scottie is no longer Scottie. And it is likely Hitchcock is also commenting sarcastically on the view that one thing art can "do" is make us better, healthier, etc.

114.   It is not out of the question that with Midge leaving, Hitchcock signals that we lose our last link to something like a traditional Hitchcockian tonality: detached, musing, ironic, somewhat clinical, with indications of a great deal of passion boiling away under the icy reserve. The conversations between Scottie and Midge have the tone of those between Lisa and Jeff in *Rear Window*, and are largely what we expect in Hitchcock suspense movies. This is not a thriller, though. It is closer to

15. FINDING JUDY

The next scene opens on a high-angle pan of all of San Francisco, left to right. Given that we will see Scottie going to four different Madeleine-associated places, it is as if Hitchcock is suggesting that Scottie will *look* for her everywhere, all over the large expanse of the city. Looking for her, which is what he appears to be doing, is, of course, a strange thing to do. He is out of the hospital and seems functional again, but his visiting these places is conducted in a way that seems nearly delusional. That is, he visits her old apartment building, where he gets excited upon seeing her old (light-green) Jaguar and its blonde female owner, and asks its new owner, animatedly, where she got it, as if there might be some link back to Madeleine; Ernie's, where he sits at exactly the same spot, and looks at "her" table from the exact same angle, and is for a second excited when he sees a blonde, well-dressed woman coming toward him, who turns out, of course, not to be Madeleine; then the museum and Carlotta's portrait, where his strange anticipation of running into Madeleine has lessened (the young woman at the portrait is a brunette); and finally the flower shop, a brief scene with no intimation at all that a living link with Madeleine might be possible. That is, he is not merely visiting her old haunts, trying to remember her. He seems unusually susceptible to the impossible suggestion that he might *see* her, and that has to mean that she might still be alive, or even that she never died. So Scottie has been ironically "twinned" with Carlotta. Just as she wandered San Francisco searching for her stolen child, so Scottie wanders the streets searching for a Madeleine he (ostensibly) knows is dead.

As with the dream, there are indications that we can see apparently better than he yet can, or that he cannot see clearly, that he is dissatisfied with the now commonly accepted description of what happened, that an insane woman committed suicide. And so he seems to be investigating, for want of a better word, although by the fourth stop his hopes seem to be flagging. (In general, just how commonly accepted act descriptions get to

---

something like a noir melodrama, and with Midge gone, there is no more element of humor, whimsy, or joking in the movie. There is plenty of irony, but it is ever darker.

be that way is also something continuously problematized by the film. Not for the vast majority of quotidian interactions, but in some events of significance, the possibilities for the manipulation of how things seem, and the cleverness of rhetoric seized on by those who have a stake in the acceptance, make for all sorts of strategies, and I think we are given hints that somewhere the tiniest of bells are going off in Scottie's mind, although it will take a while and a dramatic revelation for this all to come out.)

But then he sees a brunette in a tight green (of course) knit dress, talking with three other women, and he begins to follow her as the distinctive Madeleine musical theme begins, something we would not normally notice on a first viewing, but it is already a signal of sorts to the attentive viewer. He sees her go into the Hotel Empire (the name a faint, subtle reminder of the origins of the Carlotta story, as told by Pop Leibel, in colonialism and so to the freedom and the power of those days, which Scottie will himself begin to make some use of to get what he wants) and after some pained hesitation he follows.

Then there is an extraordinary scene. There is no indication that the woman (whom we will soon learn is Judy Barton, from Salina, Kansas) has seen Scottie, knows he is following her. When Scottie goes to her room (he has seen her at the window and knows which one it is), Judy, the Madeleine impersonator and coconspirator in murder, sees confronting her, without knowing at all what he knows, how he found her, what he wants, Scottie Ferguson, the man she set up as "the perfect witness," and the man she will insist she fell deeply in love with. She opens the door, sees him, *and does not bat an eyelash, skip a beat. Nothing* at all flickers across her face, but it must be an enormous, stunning shock to see him suddenly there (plate 17, the very first second she lays eyes on him).

She "holds" the pose of the completely-unknown-to-Scottie Judy Barton throughout the conversation, never looks uncomfortable or confused about what to do. In effect, this situation means she must now (immediately) *play* being Judy Barton as a role, that is, play the role of the "Judy who never knew Scottie."[115] And she is so expert when she is playing Madeleine

---

115.   See the discussion of *Vertigo* on this point by Wendy Doniger in *The Woman Who Pretended to Be Who She Was: Myths of Self-Imitation* (Oxford: Oxford University Press, 2005), 163–68. (In the spirit of that title, Judy might be called "The Woman Who Was Jealous of Herself.") And in Wood,

in the first part of the film that one is tempted to believe she is now deliberately *playing* a "kind of Judy who could not possibly have been Madeleine." She must be concerned that Scottie will see through the "real" Judy and see Madeleine. So it is probable to suggest that she is being deliberately coarser than she is "naturally" (if there is such a thing). And we can even speculate that when she plays the reborn Madeleine, she is careful to let enough of this (coarser, more carnal) Judy "show through," again to throw Scottie off, to prevent his concluding that no one could be this much like Madeleine.

Moreover, the film is so constantly self-referential that we should note the importance of Scottie's position. A witness is also a beholder or viewer, so Scottie's position parallels ours. He misunderstands everything he first sees, because he does not realize that it has all been staged for a certain purpose, and we miss everything that is true when we see the film for the first time. It has all been staged by Hitchcock for essentially the same reason as Elster's: to make us think Madeleine has committed suicide. What happens to Scottie in the last third of the film is also our position. Scottie notices a detail, the necklace, and he insists on and gets something like a "second viewing," one where he is much more actively interrogative, trying to put all the now confusing pieces together into one whole. That is what we, the viewers, must do as well.

In itself, though, the situation just described is not all that unusual. It happens when you are simply trying to keep someone else from knowing that you know something about him or her that he or she would rather you not know, or something that you are not supposed to know. But in this case, the stakes are so high, and the shock of Scottie showing up at her door must be so great, that we can only imagine what a struggle it must be for Judy, and how talented she is, to pull it off so flawlessly and seamlessly. It is difficult even to imagine such sangfroid, and as it goes on successfully, one begins to imagine what sense there is left, if any, of the notion of the "real" Judy Barton, whether it is rather the case that whoever Judy Barton is "onstage" at any particular time is the character calculated to be whoever is needed at that moment, with that audience. And as throughout, a second question arises, Rousseau's question introduced long ago here, whether

---

Hitchcock's Films Revisited: "The pretense was that Carlotta was taking possession of Madeleine; in reality Madeleine has taken possession of Judy" (123).

this theatricality is all that unusual; it is unusual and extreme in this case, to be sure, but it is an instance of a required dimension of modern social life that is itself not that unusual.

She is aided in all of this by the enormous class differences (or at least the differences in public class markers, the "reality" of class differences themselves being an open question) between the elegant, aloof, dreamy, spectacularly well-dressed Madeleine and the brunette, somewhat garishly dressed, working-class girl whom Scottie sees in front of him.[116] Judy has a flat Kansas accent, drops her *g*'s, and admits to being "picked up" before, and while there is an openness and honesty about the persona she presents (or the person she is; who knows?), she adopts a kind of slumping posture and a general insecure and somewhat frightened air, and there is also a slight aura of vulgarity. (So there is a Freudian twist to the "double," Judy/Madeleine, with Judy as carnal desire and sexuality and Madeleine as ego and ego ideal. If that is so, then there is a further irony in the doubling, since it suggests that the Judy/Madeleine situation is actually a figure for the duality in everyone, that everyone has a to-be-repressed "Judy" and a crafted, public "Madeleine.") And this situation gives the scene another sort of ironic twist. Without knowing it, Scottie has discovered who Madeleine "really was," and of course, he does not recognize her, does not recognize in her "his" Madeleine, and must remake her. The irony is doubled when it turns out that the new Madeleine is not a simulacrum of the original, because she *is the original*, who *was* a simulacrum created by Elster and Judy. A standard "moral of the story" for Pygmalion transformations like the one that is about to happen is that, because a person can be educated (or more often, trained) to appear like a toff, to fool even the most arrogant snob, appearances don't really matter, the exterior is not the interior, and we should assess and value (or not) only the interior. As we will see, that is not the "lesson" here. It matters if the exterior is false, a mere theatrical pose. It matters if the person feels alienated from his or her assigned exte-

---

116. The relevance of class distinctions to the general theme of deceit and self-deceit in the film would require a separate discussion. The fact that class markers are *staged*, theatrical and connected to the material gain of those who engineer them, as is the fact that Scottie's "loss" of the aristocratic Madeleine is also a gain, that he can lose that loss and so appreciate the identity between Judy and Madeleine, is discussed in Robert Pippin, "Slavoj Žižek's Hegel," in *Interanimations: Receiving Modern German Philosophy* (Chicago: University of Chicago Press, 2015), 91–116.

rior and public role, or is just playing at the Pygmalion transformation. It matters because any flourishing sociality requires that the exterior genuinely express the interior, that they be two sides of the same coin. Otherwise, trust, confidence, and any deep level of mutual understanding would be impossible. The other possible "moral of the story" in Pygmalion stories would be that the success of the transition means that a person's former "exterior" was *not* the full expression of his or her authentic "interior," that the culture, conversation, and sensibility he or she has posttransformation *is* a genuine expression of who that person really was, in potentia. This is one of the possibilities of what we are about to see, that the Madeleine Judy slowly becomes is *the Madeleine*, with all that that implies, that was "in her" all along, waiting for expression. In the second tower scene later, it is often hard to see Judy "underneath" the Madeleine who is insisting on her love for Scottie, switching easily between Judy's and Madeleine's accents. *That* Judy seems almost to disappear, not merely to be hiding behind the persona. (Of course, another possible implication of the transformation is that someone has simply been taught to be false, successfully theatrical, the kind of worry that begins to grow about Judy, when we see what a brilliant actress she is.)[117]

The point is a broad one and given full expression in Henry James's *The Portrait of a Lady*. The young Isabel Archer, idealistic, morally confident, and very, very American, and the Europeanized American woman Madame Merle, crafty, world-wise, and experienced but also a villain in the plot, had been discussing someone's ugly house. After Isabel speaks, Madame Merle makes the point relevant here, the point I think is implied by Hitchcock's treatment of similar issues, but by virtue of what he has shown us, not by virtue of what anyone has said.

> "I don't care anything about his house," said Isabel.
>
> "That's very crude of you. When you've lived as long as I you'll see that every human being has his shell and that you must take the shell into account. By the shell I mean the whole envelope of circumstances. There's no such thing as an isolated man or woman; we're each of us made up of some cluster of appurtenances.

---

117. Cf. also Cavell, from *The World Viewed*: "The modern Pygmalion reverses his exemplar's handling of his desire, and turns his woman to stone" (86).

What shall we call our 'self'? Where does it begin? where does it end? It overflows into everything that belongs to us—and then it flows back again. I know a large part of myself is in the clothes I choose to wear. I've a great respect for things! One's self—for other people—is one's expression of one's self; and one's house, one's furniture, one's garments, the books one reads, the company one keeps— these things are all expressive."

This was very metaphysical; not more so, however, than several observations Madame Merle had already made. Isabel was fond of metaphysics, but was unable to accompany her friend into this bold analysis of the human personality. "I don't agree with you. I think just the other way. I don't know whether I succeed in expressing myself, but I know that nothing else expresses me. Nothing that belongs to me is any measure of me; everything's on the contrary a limit, a barrier, and a perfectly arbitrary one. Certainly the clothes which, as you say, I choose to wear, don't express me; and heaven forbid they should!"

"You dress very well," Madame Merle lightly interposed.

"Possibly; but I don't care to be judged by that. My clothes may express the dressmaker, but they don't express me. To begin with it's not my own choice that I wear them; they're imposed upon me by society."

"Should you prefer to go without them?" Madame Merle enquired in a tone which virtually terminated the discussion.[118]

Given Judy's knowingness and Scottie's unknowingness, an undercurrent of irony suffuses the conversation. (Early on, when Judy is responding to his claim that she reminds him of someone, she says, "You saw me and something clicked." Scottie replies, "Boy, you are not far wrong." In fact she is not wrong at all, and she must know what she is saying.) But irony aside, her new persona allows them to have a conversation far different than any we saw between Scottie and Madeleine. Neither one of them ever discussed, in the ordinary sense, "who they were," their past histories, their current interests, in effect, their lives. But now, Judy can tell him "who she

118.   Henry James, *The Portrait of a Lady* (New York: Norton, 1995), 61. James is also here referring back to the book's stately opening pages, which emphasize in great detail, and with a clear sense of the weighty importance of doing so, the Touchet country house. This is a prelude to a brief conversation about whether one can "see" an interesting idea. The implication of the whole novel, and of all film, is that the answer is yes.

FIG. 27

is," even, she says, again knowingly, if she has to "prove it," which she does
by showing him her driver's license. She even spells out her Kansas license
number, one of the few times in a film someone will insist, in effect, "I am a
number, *this* number!" (figure 27). (Scottie didn't ask her to prove that she
was who she said she was; all he asked was that she tell him about herself.
A slightly defensive reaction by Judy, but no harm done, no suspicions
aroused. Apparently.)

Scottie is about to leave when he sees photographs of Judy's mother and
father, and when she shows him the photos, he seems moved, almost as if
he were now getting a chance to learn something he never learned from
Madeleine, at least part of the picture of "who someone is," the context
we need to understand someone, from where she was born and raised, to
the fact that her new stepfather made her uncomfortable,[119] and she decided to try her luck in "sunny California." Scottie again seems ready to
leave, but cannot give up this connection—what Judy looks like—to his
Madeleine. He asks her out to dinner and she agrees. (On second viewing,

119.   When she shows Scottie the picture of her father in front of his hardware store, the last "e" is
covered by the pitchfork he is holding (itself a reference to *American Gothic* by Grant Wood), and
the "Hard" is cropped from the frame, so he is standing in front of "Barton's War." Thanks to Susan
Levine.

FIG. 28

nearly everything becomes ironic, a reference to something else. Her simple request for a full hour "to change and get fixed up"—something that describes what will happen in the remainder of the movie—is such a remark.)

Scottie leaves, and it is only now, nearly an hour and forty minutes into the film, 108 minutes into a 129-minute movie, that the first-time viewer learns the truth about the Elster plot and who Judy is.[120] In a strange move, Hitchcock films Judy from the rear, and has her turn and look over her shoulder almost directly into the camera, at the viewer, at least as close as she can come without staring directly at the camera (figure 28).

The screen lighting turns red, and we see the same part of the movie we have seen before, but this time completed by a scene we did not see, and that, retrospectively, changes everything we have seen, in the way that retrospective views always do. We see Elster tossing the corpse of his wife off the tower (literally "throwing her away"), and Judy, dressed as Madeleine,

120.   In teaching the film, I have found that often well over half the students do not realize that Judy is the Madeleine Elster they came to know, or they recognize that Kim Novak is playing both roles but wonder why she is portraying two different women. There is no other moment in the film, perhaps in all of film, where one wishes as intensely that one could remember what one thought when one first saw this scene, or could see the film again, unknowing, and experience this moment for the first time, again.

has screamed, so Elster covers her mouth and wrestles her, struggling, out a side door (plate 18).

Hitchcock must realize that even with this visual reenactment, many viewers will be confused, so he adds another explanation, this time discursively. Judy sits down to write Scottie a farewell letter, in preparation for packing her suitcase and leaving. ("And so you found me. This is the moment I've dreaded and hoped for.") Explaining the plot, why she was chosen, why he was chosen, the "mistake" she made in falling in love with him, the yearning she has that he love her, she says she only wanted to see him just once more, and she has. "Now I'll go and you can give up your search." (An odd word. How did Judy know Scottie did not just happen on her in the street, but had been "searching"? Even more, why would she call it a search, if, as she must assume, Scottie believed Madeleine was dead? What does she already sense from her very brief encounter with Scottie?) She admits that if she had the nerve, she would stay and lie, hoping he would love her—and here the "metaphysics" that James mentioned begins—"as I am, for myself. And so forget the other and forget the past." After saying she doesn't know if she has the nerve to try, she rises in a way that signals she has decided she might have the nerve, tears up the letter, and puts her clothes and suitcase back in the closet. She puts at the back of the closet the gray suit she was supposed to have died in (and that she obviously kept as a souvenir, a theme that will return) and takes out a kind of anti-Madeleine dress, something it is hard to imagine Madeleine wearing, a lilac dress, rather cheap looking (figure 29). (It is a wonderful touch by Hitchcock to have Judy, after she has put away the Madeleine dress, hug her own dress close to her, embodying her desire to be, and to be taken to be, "herself.")

The film cuts to Ernie's, and occupies the same viewing angle as when we first saw Madeleine, and the camera pans left to right the same way, although, now, Judy is in the foreground and we see her first from the side (figure 30). She notices that Scottie is taken aback when a blonde woman in a gray suit enters, and there is a look of sadness on her face, as she no doubt realizes the devastation she has wrought in Scottie, and how her own relation to him will always be deeply intertwined with Madeleine's story and her likeness to Madeleine. But she has resolved to risk a great deal, banking on the fact that since she is in fact "*the* woman Scottie fell in love with," she can "make him" love her, the same her, again.

FIG. 29

FIG. 30

When Scottie brings her home, he asks her to quit her job and let him "take care of her," something that of course sounds like a proposal to be his mistress. She says no, that she understands what he is asking (she has "understood" since she was seventeen), but he promises there will be no expectations of that ("not very complimentary either," she notes), and she agrees. When they are discussing the basis for this whole relationship, that

Judy resembles Madeleine a great deal, we see her profile in the silhouette noted before, and so can call to mind his first, deep infatuation with her profile in Ernie's. As noted, the profile is "blank," apparently from his point of view, a blank slate on which he can reinscribe Madeleine, Judy as Madeleine (plates 8 and 9).

Then begins a "courtship" of some strange sort; at least a preparation for Scottie's plea to let him make her over. They stroll like young lovers along the side of a pond at the Palace of Fine Arts, with Judy noticing a couple kissing, suggesting that she must wonder why that hasn't happened between them, and revealing that she is somewhat sad about it. They dance at a fancy restaurant, Judy laying her head on his chest, Scottie noticeably wooden and unresponding. He buys her a flower at a shop on the street, across from which is the department store Ransohoff's, where, he tells the surprised Judy, he wants to buy her some clothes. He does not tell her he wants to remake her as Madeleine, but by her discomfort, her preferences for non-Madeleine clothes, and of course her memory of what Madeleine wore, she quickly realizes this, and squirms at Scottie's intense, uncompromising single-mindedness. (This is all preceded by, for once, Scottie buying her at the stand the small white flower *that she likes*, a contrasting prelude for the many times we are about to see when Scottie rather ruthlessly ignores her preferences.) In the first scene, when Scottie is trying to find Madeleine's gray suit, and is rejecting ones that Judy says she likes, Hitchcock shoots the scene in a way to emphasize the flower, as if to emphasize how much of "Judy" is being ignored in these scenes and throughout the remaking (figure 31). There is the usual irony here too. The saleswoman says that "the gentleman certainly knows what he wants," but we will see soon that Scottie admits that he doesn't at all know the point of the attempted transformation, why he believes that having created someone who looks like Madeleine, but is not, will be in any sense satisfying, rather than painful, confusing, a silly piece of theater. The question of the role of fantasy is being raised again, the kind of fantasy that is powerful enough to be confused with the real, despite what reason decrees about the real.

Judy is aware that he is looking for Madeleine's suit, and she says she "won't do it," gets off the couch, and makes as if to bolt. He follows her to a corner and does not really try to persuade her to go through with this; he simply insists on it, saying as an imperative, not a request, "Do this for me."

FIG. 31

This all occurs in front of a mirror (plate 19), as if to make the point with which this book begins, that there are always at least four people in a relationship. Now (as noted, there are several ways to count these personae), there is Judy as she sees herself, Judy as Scottie sees her, Scottie as Judy knew him, and this Scottie, post-Madeleine, obsessed with the past. As before, we could go on proliferating personae, but at least these four seem to be in play in filming this scene in this way, with the reflections and this geometry. (When Madeleine recounts her disturbing dream to Scottie, she describes a corridor that "was once mirrored" and "fragments of the mirror still hang there." It is a comment of sorts on the fragmented public personae of Judy Barton, in none of which can she see "see *herself*," but just "fragments.")

16. THE TRANSFORMATION

In the next scene, in Scottie's apartment, Judy is sitting at his desk, her head on her arms, crying. Scottie pours her a drink, and she asks, "Why are you doing this? What good will it do?" And as noted before, Scottie honestly answers, "I don't know, I don't know. No good, I guess. I don't know." Philosophically, we want to say, there must *be* a reason, an end that these means, transforming Judy, will serve, but it is not available to Scottie, not one he is in control of or conscious of. Otherwise all of this would finally not be something he is doing, but something that is happening to him, a compulsion far stronger than any metaphor. The frenzy and intensity of Stewart's performance come close several times to suggesting this, but never declare or show it. Whatever he is doing is somehow motivated, even if irrationally motivated.[121] We want to say that he doesn't know this consciously, but he wants to bring Madeleine back to life and so re-create his love, but that makes little sense, since he knows it is Judy, not Madeleine, and he will always know that. Still, doing things for reasons that don't make conscious sense is not all that unusual, although we usually have some strategy for making these actions seem to make sense. Perhaps, if we return to what was suggested in the dream sequence, the unconscious reason is to demonstrate that Judy actually *is* Madeleine, the woman who dressed as and pretended to be Madeleine, assuming that Scottie has some vague sense that no one could look that much like Madeleine, and in light of his own un-thought-through doubts about what happened. On the other hand, perhaps Scottie genuinely does not have any determinate reason for transforming Judy. Perhaps he is exploring what he wants out of the transformation by doing it. (We will see when the transformation is complete that "what he wanted," it turned out, was passionate sexual intimacy with Judy. But even that hardly seems like a full description. That end does not seem foremost in his mind now.) We want to say that he is *compelled* to try to re-create Madeleine, but his actions are not anything like someone not aware of what he is doing and why. "No good" and "I don't know" seem pretty accurate.

The ironies continue. Scottie repeats Judy's phrase to him when she was Madeleine, saying to her, "There's something in you," just as she had said, "There's something in me that wants me to die." Scottie leaves the phrase ominously unfinished. She says, "Couldn't you like me, just me, the way I am?" And she agrees to "wear the darn clothes" if he will just like her. But Scottie, a perfect mirror image of Madeleine's trances, is al-

---

121. See David Pears, *Motivated Irrationality* (Oxford: Clarendon, 1984), for a clarifying essay on the very concept.

ready off somewhere else (the theme music begins), looking at her brown hair. "The color of your hair . . ." prompts another pained reaction from Judy. Scottie, in another naïve confusion of the inner-outer dialectic, one that recalls Isabel's words quoted above, beseeches her, "Judy, please, it can't matter to you." He implies that it is just a few clothes and a new color and style for her hair; a mere outside, it will not change her inside. But Judy knows that this is simplistic, and we know that if the change is so trivial and meaningless, why is Scottie obsessed with it? He wants far more than an outside transformation, but clearly does not yet know what that is, and she is fully aware of what more he wants. Perhaps she is also afraid (it would be a reasonable fear) that the more accurately he remakes her, the less plausible it will be that Judy and Madeleine are two different people.[122] There is a strong hint of this anxiety as they move closer to the fire and Scottie, exactly as he had done the first time Madeleine was in the apartment, throws a pillow on the floor in the same spot that he had thrown it then, and they occupy the same positions with respect to each other. Judy is obviously distressed as the scene plays out, perhaps also because she knows that the only way Scottie "will love her" is on terms that are fantastical and unreal. But she is willing to try. "If I let you change me, will that do it?" she asks, seeking a kind of bargain no one can make. "Will you love me?" And Scottie says yes, he will.

Judy's invocations of "who I really am," "loving her for herself," touch on the self-other dynamics I have been tracking in the film. We know that doing whatever is necessary to make yourself desirable to the other has some sort of limit, a limit achieved very early on in most romances. You may succeed, but if you succeed too well, if the artifice is too good an artifice, you fail. This is the same irony we see in Scottie's transformation: the moment he transforms Judy into Madeleine, he fails, because he can then see that Madeleine is and was *Judy*. His bliss lasts only a few minutes. On the other hand, though, her plea to be loved "as she is," "for herself," can

---

122.   The intriguing, contrary, and also quite plausible hypothesis that Judy wants (or half knowingly wants) Scottie to slowly transform her into Madeleine, yet again reversing the active and passive roles, is suggested by William Rothman in "Scottie's Dream, Judy's Plan, Madeleine's Revenge," in Makkai, *Vertigo*. It is also possible that from the very first time Scottie saw Judy in the street, both he and she knew, or half knew, who each of them "really" was, and are both trying to find some way of acknowledging such a disturbing fact.

only mean: Can't you just love me, the woman who conspired with Elster to murder his wife, who tricked you into being a witness, who made love to you, deceived you, manipulated that love, and absconded afterward, leaving you a broken shell of what you once were? Couldn't you love *that* me? Her "project" in all of this is as tragically impossible as his, as impossible as recovering someone dead, visiting the past, forgetting the past. I mean "tragically" seriously and will come back to that point.

All of this isn't to say that the makeover scenes are not disturbing, or that Scottie's bullying is treated in the slightest as sympathetic. The whole sequence is as brutal and unadorned a view of the projection of the fantasies of male desire onto a woman treated as mere object, screen, occasion for his projection, as there exists in cinema. Nor is the pathos and sadness with which Judy must submit (or risk losing Scottie again) ever undercut or qualified.

That beauty parlor scene is very redolent with Hollywood images, preparing stars for their star turn in the film, manufacturing a look, as Hitchcock invokes again the similarity between our susceptibility for, desire for, fantasy and the control of appearances and the movie world. The music from the opening credits, repetitive, and highly suggestive of suspense, sounds again. The language has shifted from "the gentleman certainly knows what he wants" (but we saleswomen don't and must find it) to a full acceptance of the transformation; from the cosmetologist: "Yes, sir, we know what you want."[123]

Scottie is back in the apartment, waiting fitfully for "his Madeleine" to appear. She finally does. He sees her in the hall and watches as she walks toward him. She is still Judy in demeanor if not in her physical appearance. Tentative, nervous, a bit rueful at what she has agreed to. She must know the hair is wrong, but we feel for her as she tries to save one slim element of her "real self." She wears her hair down, similar to how Judy wore it. He wants it up and off her face (perhaps we remember that Midge, also trying to be what Johnny wants, in her anger pulls her hair back and off her face), and Judy defends herself by claiming that that look didn't seem to suit her.

123. Trumpener points out that neither the saleswoman nor the cosmetologist seems at all surprised that a man would want to remake a woman according to *his* standards of beauty, no matter what the woman keeps insisting she wants. Trumpener, "Fragments of the Mirror," 184.

But of course she realizes that this is hopeless. Suiting her is not what this is all about. She knows this is the last step, and she knows what his reaction will be, what will happen to her, when the transformation is complete and there will be virtually no way to keep up the fiction of her separate identity. They are in effect negotiating the terms of their relationship, with both of them eager to control those terms, as if they could, Judy by resisting, Scottie by demanding. But Judy cannot really tell herself that she is withholding the final piece of the transformation so as to retain some meager control over her own identity, because by becoming Madeleine again, she *becomes what she was*, the fake Madeleine. There is nothing she can do about that, or even that part of her. What we have seen and will see indicates that it would be simplistic to think she is simply impersonating Madeleine again when she comes out of the bathroom. Whoever Madeleine seemed to be to Scottie was, to use the phrase we have heard twice before, "in her," in the way she can wear those clothes and pull it off, her general bearing, the upper-crust accent, the elegant control of her demeanor and language. If we have understood anything at all about the movie, we should have understood that thinking that all of that is *merely* "external," with the corresponding illusion that there is a separable, core true self "inside" that one privately knows and controls, is of a piece with all the other fantasies the characters embrace. Madeleine is now and always was some version of Judy, of who Judy is. This is not to say that the ambition to be oneself and not who one is taken to be is foolish or hopeless. It is a deeply frustrating thing if one feels that one is being taken to be someone who one is not, and one is right to struggle against it. But the terms of that struggle are endlessly complicated, as we have seen with Scottie (if he succeeds in re-creating Madeleine, he will get not just an exterior that he can fantasize is Madeleine; he will get the inner of *that* outer, Judy expressing herself as the Madeleine she can be, and that, obviously, is not his fantasy) and with Madeleine (if she consoles herself that it is just a costume, she will be self-deceived; the costumed Madeleine was and is, after all, Judy).

The Wagnerian theme starts sounding again as Judy is in the bathroom, fixing her hair, and the strings speed up, the phrases repeat and repeat and repeat, and then begin slowly to build to a climax. We get the anxious sensation that we get in a five-hour Wagnerian opera, that the theme introduced long ago in the overture is about to resolve itself climactically, just as

we sense right before the "Liebestod." One could say that since the opening chase, we have been carried along by the music in perpetual *suspension*,
and are about either to climb down or to fall down. (This feature recalls
Scottie's predicament, hanging from the rain gutter. Because we don't see
that or how he gets down, the entire movie, as Wood suggests, could be
said to exist in suspension, musical and otherwise.)[124] Judy's entrance into
the bedroom is one of the finest and most powerful, if also fully dreamlike
and fantastical, scenes Hitchcock ever filmed. Scottie has his back to the
camera, hears the bathroom door open, and turns as the music swells. The
green light (from the Hotel Empire marquis outside), the color of mystery,
of the unknown (equally appropriate for the mysteries of romantic love as
for the simply unknowable that we still need to know), suffuses the room
from behind Scottie. When Hitchcock cuts from Scottie to Madeleine, the
full force of the musical theme we have been intermittently hearing is at its
highest volume and most intense and is resolved the moment we see Judy-
now-fully-Madeleine, so bathed in the green light that we can barely make
her out at first. One of the many extraordinary elements of the scene is the
expression on Kim Novak's face as she purposely and confidently walks
forward, with none of the hesitations, tentativeness, and somewhat whiny
traits of Judy. Those are gone. She not only knows she is Madeleine; she
clearly knows (we see she knows) that she now possesses infinitely more
power in the relationship than she would ever have as Judy (figure 32 and
plate 20). The subtlety of Novak's performance reaches its apogee here.
She manages to convey somehow that *this* Madeleine is one where Judy
is still visible playing the role, not wholly effaced. Madeleine's face has the
open, yearning, and very American expression that we recognize as Judy's,
even as she also clearly realizes the fact that she is not an imitation of Scottie's Madeleine; she is all the Madeleine there ever was.[125]

Scottie is finally able to embrace and kiss "his" Madeleine, and holds
her face in his hands as the camera appears to glide 360 degrees around
them.[126] (Another spiral that moves, but only as revolving around its fixed

124. Wood, *Hitchcock's Films Revisited*, 111.
125. See Harvey's description in *Movie Love in the Fifties*, 39.
126. They were on a revolving turntable (which ironically caused some genuine vertigo problems
for Stewart) and the background images were transparencies. See Auiler, *"Vertigo,"* 119.

FIG. 32

origin.) Contrary to the first kiss at the beach, this scene is not undercut but *thoroughly* romanticized by the score, and the only irony comes from our knowing that the person Scottie thinks is the theatrical Madeleine whom he created is the real Madeleine, that is, Judy's fake Madeleine. The scene is clearly intended to, and largely does, sweep *us* away too in a brief moment of relief and emotional release. Perhaps we are swept away because the desire to re-create the erotic power of a past is not just a neurotic obsession of one character. The relation between or the great tension between romantic love, the beginnings of a relationship, and companionate marital love, its future, is an important theme in Hitchcock's films, paradigmatically in *Rear Window*, and the rituals in marital love that seek to re-create the original romantic love are testimony to the power of this fantasy in everyday life.[127] We know Scottie is still deceived, and we sense that something catastrophic will happen soon, but we are invited to, and we largely do, indulge ourselves in the passion of the moment. How could we not? It is the most devoutly wished in any human fantasy: overcoming death itself, bringing a loved one who has died back to life. Typical of Hitchcock, we can identify

---

127. Not to mention the relevance of the issue early on in Hitchcock's career, in *The Thirty-Nine Steps* and its closing scene with its suggestion that marriage can seem a self-handcuffing. Cf. Stanley Cavell, "North by Northwest," *Critical Inquiry* 7, no. 4 (Summer 1981): 767.

with Scottie's ecstatic experience—and one has to be made of stone, or consumed by cynicism, not to be carried away by this "return" to the past and to the earliest moments of their love—even while we appreciate the irony. He thinks he has created a simulacrum, a theatricalized version of Madeleine, but he has authored the *real* Madeleine, the Madeleine whom he loved, for she was a simulacrum played by the same "actress," Judy.[128]

In fact, this duality, a level of emotional investment that can coexist with a realization of the subterfuges and deceptions, is a feature of the film as a whole. That is, many viewers, including this one, will report that, even knowing what they know about the murder plot, even after fifteen or twenty viewings, they are drawn into the romance plot in the first half of the movie, and still deeply sympathetic to Scottie after the apparent suicide of Madeleine. Watching the film several more times does not "destroy" the illusions that made the first viewing first. Our responses and involvement are largely the same. This is, in part, testimony to the persistence of the aspiration for romantic love still very much alive in the contemporary world. In fact, even the film's devastating picture of the dangerous implications of the romantic love mythology can coexist unproblematically with those very aspirations. I think that this is one of the many reasons so many people also report that they found the film "disturbing." We sense that difference noted by Bernard Williams, between what we think we think and what we actually think.

But as mentioned, Scottie's moment of bliss, all of it a fantasy, cannot last long and it does not. Even during the kiss itself, Scottie seems to remember that this kiss feels *exactly* like the one in the stables and he even imagines the stables; we see what he is imagining as the camera moves around, and the music changes (figure 33). And of course this would happen. The feel of Madeleine's particular body in his arms, the texture of her

128.   This is a theme Hitchcock introduces in several films. Perhaps the most interesting example, aside from *Vertigo*, is its role in *Psycho* and the many questions *Psycho* raises but does not answer. When Norman "is" his mother, does he (Norman) know that Mother has taken over his body? Does he resist? When he is Mother, does he, qua Mother, know he is also still Norman? Does he, Norman, think the corpse is his mother and that she comes alive as a different embodied being, not him? The final scene, with Mother triumphant, convinced she has pinned the murders on her son, Norman, is even more complicated, since she seems to believe she is a stuffed corpse and cannot move, or that she can successfully pretend to be such a corpse and "fool" them.

FIG. 33

skin, her scent, her taste, the "style" of her kiss, so many things must feel exactly the same, and yet how could that be? The moment is too powerful for him to stop and reflect though, however confused he seems to be, and the kiss goes on, until all the movie conventions of the late fifties are invoked, and they clearly make love (plate 21). Their conversation in the next scene is clearly postcoital.

17. THE REVELATION

In this happy aftermath, both of them cheerful, even ebullient, Judy/Madeleine expresses a preference for dinner, Ernie's of course ("after all, it's our place," she says, probably saying more than she means to, a first indication that she might get careless), and they banter back and forth while she finishes dressing. Then, acting on what must be an unconscious or semiconscious *wish* to be discovered (perhaps some concession to what she really wants, to be loved as she is, just for herself; for this is what she was and is, *that* woman in the Elster plan), she puts on a necklace she has saved from the murder scheme, one that Elster no doubt had created to match the one in the painting, supposed to invoke Carlotta (plate 22).

It is hard to imagine her making such a mistake without some other motive involved. She was cautious enough to hide Madeleine's signature gray suit in the back of her closet, and she has seemed rightly nervous about being made over to look *too* much like Madeleine (the last instance of which was her returning home with her hair down), but I assume we are to think that she is so overjoyed to be able to "love" Scottie again, that she throws caution to the wind. Madeleine, after all, never wore the necklace, and the odds of someone remembering what jewelry in a painting looks like are slim. But, on the other hand, she knows Scottie is a detective. She is a confederate of Elster's, and Scottie's accident while on the force is part of the plan. The gesture has to be counted, in some sense, as pathological. Remarkably, she even says to him as he fumbles with the clasp: "Can't you see?" Indeed.[129]

Scottie recognizes the necklace (we have been "primed" for this, that he would remember, by its appearance in his dream), and the camera zooms up to his concerned expression. The Carlotta theme sounds as he notices it, this time with horns. At the very moment when she has lost Scottie, and indeed the very moment when he loses her as Madeleine (he immediately conceives the plan of driving to the mission, and he changes their dinner plans, suggesting they go out of town, knowing there can only be one explanation for her having the necklace), she says, "Scottie, I do have you now, don't I?"

18. "I LOVED YOU SO, MADELEINE"

The drive to San Juan Bautista mirrors in very many details the earlier drive there for the fake suicide, except it is dark. But Judy/Madeleine is now much more nervous. Their roles have been reversed. She had engineered the first trip (by making him think he proposed it), and was in effect the one running the show, active, with Scottie passive. On this drive, although

---

129.   The fact that it only takes a second for Scottie to put together immediately the necklace with the death is another hint that he was primed for this in some way, had some inkling, as I have been suggesting. See also Patrick Brion, *Hitchcock: Biographie, filmographie illustré, analyse critique* (Paris: Éditions de La Martinière, 2000), 517.

she suspects something, she is not yet able to see that Scottie is now running the show. He knows that something about the suicide was illusory,
and that something overall is very wrong, and he is taking her back to the
mission for the truth, and perhaps much more. We have not really been
prepared for Scottie to kill Judy in revenge for what she did to him, but
we have seen his bullying as he made her over, and we have already been
profoundly surprised twice by the film, by the suicide and then by Judy's
revelation that it was a murder. We are unsure what he plans. As she too
notices the scenery, it becomes clear to her where they are going, and she
asks nervously about their destination. Scottie tells here, "One more thing
I have to do, then I'll be free of the past." (Another fantasy. He is in effect
ensuring that he will never escape the past.) We don't know what he plans
to do (and our concern will grow as he hauls her up the bell tower), but as
he says these words, a strange, somewhat malicious smile appears on his
face, and he seems almost smug, satisfied perhaps that he has stumbled on
the truth, "solved the case," as it were.

As he drags her, resisting and trying to wrestle away, he tells her that he
couldn't get up the stairs the first time, but she's his "second chance." (His
second chance is also the occasion for another Hitchcockian doubling. In
wrestling a struggling Judy at the top of the stairs, he is doubling Elster's
role in the murder, reinforcing their twin roles as directors of the drama
[figures 34 and 35].) So we wonder if the one more thing he has to do is
actually to get all the way up the stairs with his made-over Judy ("I need
you to be Madeleine for a little while"), reenacting the original event, but
with him successfully climbing to the top this time (and, if he is going to
literally double Elster's role, throwing her off). That's what he tells Judy,
but he clearly has in mind forcing her to confront the scene of the crime,
no doubt expecting that he can make her explain how it was all done. His
tone is aggressive, slightly sarcastic, full of contempt, and certain to the
point of arrogance. As he forces her up the stairs (calling her Judy all the
while), the suspense music keeps alternating with the Madeleine theme,
producing an amazing effect, somehow reminding us that underneath the
appearances we are seeing, and so the apparent danger to Judy, and despite
the aggression and confidence and willfulness, Scottie's heart is broken
still. The pull of his love for Madeleine and the intensity of his desperation
are all still as alive as ever.

As they go higher, the vertigo occurs again, twice (we see the vertigo

FIG. 34

FIG. 35

effect, the zooming-forward-while-pulling-the-camera-backward shot, down the stairwell), but Scottie has no trouble now going to the top. (He could not save Madeleine, or prevent the policeman from dying, so love and ordinary solicitude were not motive enough, but his rage at being betrayed is strong enough to get him up the tower. It will be clear soon that part of that rage involves a humiliation at the hands of Elster, that his anger has

FIG. 36

something to do with some sort of competition he notes between him and Elster.) He tells Judy that he recognized the necklace, and forces her to tell him all the details. She admits her role, and it is clear that Scottie's rage has little to do with the real Mrs. Elster's death, but with a lover's betrayal. "He made you over, just like I made you over." And then the competitive note just mentioned sounds. "Only better. Not only the clothes and the hair, but the looks and the manner and the words. And those beautiful phony trances..." (figure 36). In the midst of his tirade and manhandling of Judy, he notices that he has climbed to the top and his mood breaks for a second. "I made it. I made it," he says. "We're going up to look at the scene of the crime."

At the top, Scottie sounds the note we have heard before, "With all his wife's money, and all that freedom and that power, he ditched you." (Again the resonance with "he threw her away" from Pop Leibel.) But as he explains to Judy that the necklace gave her away, and tells her that she shouldn't have been that sentimental, his voice breaks saying that word, the mood of the scene changes, and we hear for the last time, the lovely and elegant Madeleine theme. He then utters probably the saddest line in the movie. After everything that has happened, and everything he has learned, one thing still overwhelms his bitterness and anger at being betrayed: "I loved you so, Madeleine." This said to a woman he had been calling Judy until this moment, revealing again the power of the romantic fantasy he had created in the first part of the film.

Speaking, I suppose, only for myself, I find there to be an almost unearthly power in what amounts to the beginning of an admission that the grip of a fantasy, a projected image, a theatrical persona, can survive with a life-altering intensity, even after the "truth" is known. In this case, Scottie knows that Madeleine is Judy Barton from Salina, Kansas, but "for him," she is still Madeleine. It has this power for the viewer (for some viewers) because it touches on much more than the individual character Scottie's psychological need to believe. It has much more power for the viewer than that because it touches on the impossibility of thinking of all of this as simply a matter of what was pretense and what is now revealed to be truth. To say that there was as much of Judy in Madeleine (recall the rather frank and steady look on "Madeleine's" face when, naked, she pretends to wake up in Scottie's bed) as there was of Madeleine in Judy is also to say that the relation between the need to believe and what we believe is, when it comes especially to romantic love, not rightly thought of as simply a matter of wishful thinking and delusion. "What we need to believe" also involves matters of hope, trust, staking things on faith in someone, and what we believe is not just statable as a proposition, but is intertwined with many unavoidable factors that go into the thick description of such a content. This gets another turn of the screw in the film because Scottie's statement touches on what we continue to believe and especially to feel, no matter how many times we tell ourselves, as we tear up at the line, that it is "only a movie," or it is just Scottie's pathology again, and so forth. Hitchcock understands that there is a truth in the fantasies he knows how to create and sustain that is unaffected by our knowing that what we have seen is "not real."

Judy sees an opening for at least a conversation about all of this. She tells him she was safe when he found her, that she still loves him, that she let him change her because she loves him, and pleads, in effect, for forgiveness and reconciliation. He tells her, using the same phrase she had in the first stable scene, that it's "too late," that "there's no bringing her back," and we think we might be hearing our first moment of some moral regret, that he is referring to the real, dead Madeleine. Then we realize that he means there is no bringing back the illusory Madeleine, no way to re-create his fantasy figure. But as she begs him, "please," they kiss in a way that betrays no reluctance on Scottie's part (plate 23), and that seems to mark a shift, as if he would eventually forgive her. No doubt that is unlikely, but we are not permitted to find out what might happen after the kiss. Looking over his shoulder, again as she had done in the first stable scene, she sees a spectral dark figure climbing the stairs toward them, recoils in fright, steps off the ledge, and falls to her death. The last words we hear in the film are "I heard voices" and "God have mercy." (The last perhaps a suggestion of what Scottie was about to bestow?) The camera withdraws into a point of view from empty space outside the tower, and the film ends with Scottie on the edge of the tower, looking down at the body of Judy (plate 24). We don't know if he is poised to jump himself, something at least hinted at by the fact that, visually, the shot suggests a man peering down into a grave with a headstone behind him, perhaps his grave, or if he is simply horrified as he looks down at Judy's corpse. The former would mean that, of the two psychological elements in vertigo, the desire to fall, to end his misery, has won out. We have no real hint of that, or anything else in the final gesture. All we know is that forcing Madeleine up the stairs and learning the truth has cured his vertigo. But he seems somehow crushed, diminished forever, by being "cured." The strange position of his hands could bear scores of different meanings, and everything is left open. The most poignant interpretation, and I think the most likely, is that it is the pose of a man whose outstretched arms have failed to catch something falling, pulled back, and who looks on in shock at the results. So much for his second chance; it essentially repeats the results of the first chance, this time because of mere chance.

And there is a last irony. Scottie has now done what he kept promising he could do throughout the film, find a rational explanation for everything. "There is an answer for everything." "If I could just find the key." "Don't you see, you've given me something to work with." He now knows the truth behind the "phony trances" and the earlier fake suicide attempt in the bay, but it is a calamitous truth for him, nothing he could have ever imagined. He has put it all together, but it has landed him here, alone, bereft, if also "cured" of vertigo. It is certainly not the case that Hitchcock is somehow suggesting that behind every romantic fantasy there is evil, deception, betrayal, and the like, and that once we are cured of the vertiginous illusions of romantic love, our situation will be like Scottie's. But in the first place, Hitchcock often acknowledges that there *is* sometimes a huge cost to be paid for uncovering what lies beneath the tangled deceptions, illusions, and general indifference and ignorance that attend ordinary appearances. Young Charlie discovers that cost in *Shadow of a Doubt*, Jeff discovers it in *Rear Window*, Arbogast in *Psycho* has to pay that price, Mark Rutland in *Marnie* discovers it when he forces his way into Marnie's inner life and learns the truth, and there are many other instances. And there are other options available in Hitchcock's films. Some characters are aware of this distinction between real and apparent, but do not do much, if anything, to challenge it. Guy Haynes in *Strangers in a Train* is a good example of this. Devlin, Cary Grant's character in *Notorious*, is also such a type. There are some who deny the distinction, and insist on the classical sophistical position, like Roger in *North by Northwest*. (Hence the play on his middle initial, "O," which, he says, stands for nothing, suggesting he is nothing, but only what he wants himself to appear to be.)[130] And sometimes characters do not notice the distinction at all. The citizens of Santa Rosa in *Shadow of a Doubt* would count as such, especially given the painful irony of the minister's excessively laudatory funeral oration in the closing scene of that film about a serial killer. Bruno's mother in *Strangers on a Train* is the most ludicrous example of such blindness, willful or not. The cost in Scottie's case is enormous, but he has been "cured" of his vertigo. He has the consolation of the truth, and is freed from his fantasy, but the last scene sounds no consoling cinematic note.

This suggests a tragic dimension to the end of the movie. In the world of unknowingness created by Hitchcock, we obviously cannot take things as they always seem, must struggle to distinguish the public self-representations of others and our own self-representations from what is truly the case, must work to distinguish the staged and theatrical from the real, the self-deceived from the honest. We cannot but do this, but doing so also brings with it all sorts of risks. The truth we think we see may degrade our confidence, commitment, or love. We may think we have found the truth behind an appearance, but that might be a projection rather than a discovery, needlessly ruining some relationship. (This is why, however relevant a psychoanalytic explicans is for the film, it can assume an authoritative

---

130. The actual sophistical position is deeply intertwined with the philosophical problem of nothing, or nonbeing as well, as in Plato's *Sophist*. Roger finally encounters the Real in a way that almost kills him, in the empty flatlands, alone, an "unaccommodated man," when the crop dusting plane tries to kill him.

knowingness that is also a kind of blindness. See the psychiatrist's speech in *Psycho*.) Some illusions, some fantasies, might be punctured in too sweeping and crude a way, destroying something, an aspect of which is essential to living well and especially to romantic love. Unknowingness, in other words, of the sort we have been describing is in itself a tragic situation.[131]

CONCLUDING REMARKS: MORAL SUSPENSION

The aspiration in this discussion was to show that we do not have to choose between these exclusive alternatives: in *Vertigo*, either Hitchcock has created an entertaining, erotically powerful, slightly perverse story of fantasy and betrayal, or his point in creating such a story about the role of fantasy in modern life was to show us something about that role and about romantic love in the conditions of complex interdependence and corresponding uncertainty, general unknowingness, unique to modern societies. He is clearly doing both, as he always does. What has emerged is literally a "picture," a moving picture, of our struggle to understand ourselves and each other in such a condition. Several dimensions of that picture of that struggle transcend the particularities of the strange plot. We see that the best position from which such attempts might succeed is, unfortunately, post facto, retrospectively, just as it is for Hitchcock's films. We have seen that our understanding of others is not observational, and punctual, but interpretive and extended in time; a spectatorial stance toward others is inadequate to reach any mutual understanding; an engagement with

---

131.   There are several places in his work where Nietzsche says he is out to question "the value of truth," and asks, "Why truth? Why not untruth?" This has led some to believe that he is proposing the absurd position (so it has always seemed to me) that people should decide to believe whatever it is of benefit to them to believe, or whatever is life-affirming, or whatever is yes-saying, or whatever, even if false, rather than what they know to be true. But it is impossible to will oneself to believe something because it would be good to believe it (this is otherwise known, outside some circle of Nietzsche commentators, as wishful thinking), and Nietzsche is, I would suggest, alluding to something similar to the results drawn here. A "blind" commitment to the rejection of appearances and the insistence on truth can be very dangerous because it is based on a crude duality, and because it is so subject to self-deceit or narrow moralism.

others over time is the only (slim) chance we have. We need to experience the relation between what they say and what they do, and how they understand over time what they think of themselves doing, how they come to understand what we do. (This is the main cautionary theme of *Rear Window*.) And we have seen that any such engagement is immediately a complex dialectical tangle. It can hardly just involve my understanding of you and your understanding of me. It has to involve my understanding of your understanding of me and vice versa, just as it must involve my assessment of the genuineness of your self-representation and vice versa, just as it must involve my ability to assess my own motives for understanding you and for understanding your understanding of me as I do.

This all has something to do with a peculiarity of the film I have occasionally noted throughout, something that has been present by its absence. This is the fact that, by virtue of what the characters say, what the film shows us, what seems called for in reaction to what happens, the bearing of moral judgment about the events and characters appears to have been placed in some sort of suspension, as if the judgments are available, but not somehow appropriate in this context. One example of this is prominent.

I noted previously that unknowingness and trying to learn how to deal with, live with the burden of, such unknowingness are the most prominent features of the world within which Hitchcock's characters move. But in his other films, characters *do* end up finally blaming and bringing to justice the *right* person, albeit often by accident or blind luck. It is a distinctive feature of *Vertigo* that the chief villain is not caught. That is, it is a rarity among his films. The villain is not apprehended or killed, and there are no circumstances mitigating his guilt, as in *Blackmail* or *Sabotage*. (Hitchcock resisted pressure to change the ending and did not use the alternate ending he in fact filmed, in which Midge hears on the radio that Elster has been apprehended by the authorities and is being extradited back to the States.) That lingering injustice in the final version of the film is somehow not of concern, certainly not prominent.

And in *Vertigo* especially, compared with other films, there are many more specific reasons for what appears to be a general suspension of the conditions for moral assessment (not at all of course the same thing as the suspension of moral distinctions). This is as true of Scottie's reaction (he does not seem much concerned with the murder of Elster's wife or even Judy's role in it, as much as he is about being betrayed by a lover, and by something even deeper: that he has lost Madeleine again; in fact he has lost his loss of Madeleine—there was never a "Madeleine" to lose) as it is prominent in what the viewer is expected to attend to. (I think it fair to say that our sympathies in the last third of the film are directed to Judy, even knowing that she is the murdering Judy.) Moreover, from the very beginning of their adulterous affair—for that is what it is—neither seems at all concerned with betraying the husband, Elster, who Scottie has no reason to doubt is what he seems, a loving and concerned husband. We even tend to overlook something even more disturbing. Imagine that it were true that Madeleine, his college friend's wife, was in the grip of a psychosis about being possessed (which is Scottie's first assumption) and that she was in fact entrusted to Scottie's provisional care. What could be more clearly morally objectionable than *sleeping* with such a woman? Noticing this on a subsequent viewing no doubt has something to do with our increased sensitivity to such abuse in the contemporary world, but no attention is directed to this issue in the film; there is no hesitation in Scottie's kiss by the beach.

This is of course a famous feature of great art, one which worried Plato a great deal, that we are somehow swept away by art in a way that can be ethically and morally bad for us. But that, what is good or bad *for us* in experiencing art, is a derivative issue. The first issue is why; what accounts for the fact that we feel it would be somehow churlish, simplistically moralistic, or in some way "off" for a reader to take away, say, from *Madame Bovary, Anna Karenina,* or *Effi Briest,* that these women "should have known" the wages of sin, that they "got what was coming to them," or that the most important thing we can say about them is that they were all immoral, lying, deceiving adulteresses. We do have such a response to the villains in Hitchcock films like *I Confess, Rear Window, Shadow of a Doubt,* and to Elster in this film. (Although in cinematic viewing time, we have very little chance to reassess Elster. All that must come on subsequent viewings, and of course our view of him is completely different on a second viewing.) But something about our familiarity, even intimacy with other characters, and our awareness of the fragile and uncertain self- and other-knowledge apparent all seem to reduce our confidence that we really understand the characters or even what is actually happening. Without such confidence, a moral judgment comes to feel hubristic.[132]

The intertwining in romantic contexts of what one passionately wants to see and what one actually sees plays the greatest role here. The paradigmatic example of such indeterminacy is "what Scottie intends to do" by remaking Judy into Madeleine. He wants Judy to look like Madeleine but to what end? He will always know it is not Madeleine. Recall the dialogue:

JUDY: Why are you doing this? What good will it do?
SCOTTIE: I don't know, I don't know. No good, I guess. I don't know.

As we saw, the coroner's crudely confident assessment of "what was done," and so what any one of the parties was trying to do, and who is responsible, is also a case in point.[133] Moreover, when Scottie is asked by Judy in effect to forgive her, he is called on to assess the sincerity of her present avowals in a way that is impossible. (In general, the moral point of view has a problem with forgiveness, a hard time with the question, Once some moral harm has been done, when, under what conditions does the active application of some sort of blame, some kind of "enforcement" of blame, cease to be reasonable?) Part of the reason it is impossible for Scottie to assess Judy's avowals is that there is no reason to believe that *Judy* has available to her any clear access to why she did what she did and what she feels now, or what act she is trying to prevent by saying what she does.[134]

---

132. For another cinematic example of the issue, see Robert Pippin, "Angels and Devils in Almodóvar's *Talk to Her*," in *Talk to Her*, ed. A. W. Eaton (New York: Routledge, 2009). I don't mean to suggest that Hitchcock's view of all of this is complete or definitive. Much the same situation as he describes is common in the novels of Henry James, but in that case he is particularly sensitive to what sorts of *new* moral assessments, or, more generally, new ways of holding each other to account, arise in the vertiginous situations and their modern social environments common to both Hitchcock and James. See Robert Pippin, *Henry James and Modern Moral Life* (Cambridge: Cambridge University Press, 2000).

133. This raises the question of why such a depiction of that one individual, perhaps a singularly moralistic prig, should have any *general* bearing on this issue, but Hitchcock's cinematic deflation of such thoughtless confidence is prevalent enough in his films that we can count it as part of the "world" presented by the films as a whole.

134. Some commentators at this juncture take this point to be part of another, one prominent among those who think of Hitchcock as a "Catholic" director. See Éric Rohmer and Claude Chabrol,

Second, any putative self-knowledge, avowal of intention, any insistence on a distinction between "who I am" and "the person you take me to be," presumes, especially in intimate relations where each matters to the other, some functional interdependence between my understanding of another, my understanding of his or her understanding of me, and my self-understanding, as well as assumptions about what could or could not be possible, given the other and the way he or she matters to me. The relation to another and the possible context of action shift in time, sometimes very rapidly, ensuring that any "inner insight" I might have about myself could not possibly be a punctual moment of insight, outside this fluidity.[135] This all makes aspirations of authenticity, sincerity, advice like "just be yourself," or even an insistence on being loved for "who I really am," to say the least, fraught.

Put another way, we seem to be invited by all of this to ponder the significance of Nietzsche's famous aphorism from *Beyond Good and Evil*: "Whatever is done out of love takes place beyond good and evil."[136] The aphorism seems to be saying that people in love are indifferent to moral assessment, don't care about rightness or wrongness in what they do. But that would be to misinterpret Nietzsche as well as the film. In *Beyond Good and Evil*, Nietzsche is out to show something quite relevant to Hitchcock's movie. He wants to point out first the frequent opacity in human self-knowledge, our ignorance about why we do what we do in significant choices, given how subject we are to deception, even eager to be deceived

---

Hitchcock: The First Forty-Four Films, tran. Stanley Hochman (New York: Ungar, 1979). In this extension of the account, this opacity and self-deceit is true but irrelevant because human beings are such profoundly sinful creatures that at the bottom of almost any deed there is some egoistic or otherwise corrupt motive, motives we have every reason to hide from ourselves. There are plenty of blameless characters in Hitchcock and a host of unproblematically evil villains. And while there are moments that seem like sweeping nihilistic condemnations of human beings—like the "neighbors" lament in *Rear Window*, or Uncle Charles's speech in *Shadow of a Doubt* ("Do you know the world is a foul sty? Do you know if you ripped the fronts of houses, you'd find swine?")—such views are isolated and balanced by a fundamental humanism. So there is no general skepticism about moral categories of assessment. The issue is their application in erotic romantic contexts.

135.   The general philosophical point here is that there is no way to fix the content of a subject's putative "inner experience" except by virtue of many actual and possible relations to aspects of the world "outside" such a putative inner terrain.

136.   Nietzsche, *Beyond Good and Evil*, §153, p. 70.

in some cases, and given the almost inevitable self-deceit in many of our ascriptions of motives and in the act descriptions we give. He means that this is true *especially* in cases like love, where what we interpretively see is so intertwined with our own powerful passions and with our evaluation of how others see us, that the moral psychology required by the moral point of view can no longer be said to apply. It also means for him that a strict dualism between good conduct and bad is simplistic. As noted before, he speaks often of "gradations" and of the inseparability of one category from the other, given our inability in complex cases to distinguish among over-determined motives the relevant one.[137]

In the context of this film, though, an additional topic is being introduced. Hitchcock never goes so far as to suggest that wrongs were not done, persons were not wronged.[138] There is nothing in Hitchcock's films that suggests such a conclusion, and, for example, in *I Confess*, there is no ironic qualification on a priest's courageous refusal, as a matter of moral duty, to violate the confidentiality of the confessional, even when it threatens to destroy his life. But moral standards are one thing, and confidence in their applicability another. (Even in *I Confess*, the priest is also trying to protect his former lover's identity and a blackmail plot.) And that wavering confidence can raise another question not often discussed in accounts of morality, except indirectly in treatments of forgiveness. As we have already noted, that question is not blame, but something like the "duration" of the active applicability of blame and any confidence in one's assessment. The psychological complications in *Vertigo* thus raise as a question *the point* of attempts at moral blame, and especially the question of, whatever blame can be assigned, what the point of holding someone forever accountable would be. At the end of the film, we are at the point when Scottie seems to be faced with that question, only to have the question rendered moot, giving one of the film's refrains, "it's too late," yet another of its many meanings.

137. Such a thought is not unknown in Hitchcock. The good Charlie and the evil Charles in *Shadow of a Doubt* are said to be twins, and Charlie's many remarks about their secret bond make the Nietzschean point.

138. There is no space here to discuss the larger question, that for Nietzsche these two issues are indeed linked, given the necessary role that the isolation of intentions has for the very meaning of the evaluative distinctions.

INDEX